WHAT IS DISCIPLESHIP?

Understanding the Call and Expectations of Discipleship

Highlands Church
9050 E. Pinnacle Peak Road, Scottsdale, AZ 85255
Internet: www.highlandschurch.org
Email: info@highlandschurch.org

All web links were valid at time of publication

Table of Contents

Chapter 1

DISCIPLESHIP – A Clear Command

Do you respond well to a command?

When you were growing up, were you responsive when your parents told you to clean your room? Did you immediately get to it, or was there a little procrastination between order and execution? If they told you to be home by 10:00 pm, would you faithfully make the deadline, or were you constantly pushing the envelope and making excuses on why you were late? On the job, if your boss told you to crunch the numbers on a project by Monday, would you clear your weekend to make it happen? If your spouse told you to go to the store and even gave you a list, would all of the items be dutifully checked off?

Just how do you respond to a command?

It helps when the command is clear. No ambiguity. No grey areas. Simply stated commands are the easiest to understand and easier to follow than fuzzy ones.

And it is beneficial when the one issuing the command carries the proper authority to do so. If an underling two levels down on the organizational chart issues a command to a supervisor up the chain of command, it doesn't carry as much water as the order that comes from the president's office. An order given by the boss swings a lot of weight. Can you imagine the young private who wasn't responsive, obedient, or respectful to his drill sergeant? Pity to that fool!

If one in supreme authority issues a clear command and provides every resource needed for execution, is there any reason to expect the command wouldn't be followed? Probably not - unless you're talking to the church. Because in the church world, commands issued by Jesus seem to be deemed optional by many.

[If you have access to a YouTube video – check out Francis Chan's illustration of this principle. https://www.youtube.com/watch?v=9KIA-DGx_3Y&t=1s][1]

In this first step of the discipleship journey we need to be diligent to take a close look at the clear command that Jesus gave regarding discipleship. Our foundational passage for discipleship is Matthew 28:18-20.

> 18 And Jesus came and said to them, "All authority in heaven and on earth has been given to me. 19 Go therefore and make disciples of all nations, baptizing them in the name of the Father and of the Son and of the Holy Spirit, 20 teaching them to observe all that I have commanded you. And behold, I am with you always, to the end of the age."
>
> Matthew 28: 18-20 ESV

This key passage on discipleship contains several important foundational elements that will help us frame the nature of discipleship. As we work our way through this passage, let's ask, then answer, some key questions.

The first question is "Who is speaking?" Verse 18 tells us plainly that Jesus is the one who is initiating the conversation. But reading the passage in context tells us that this is the risen Jesus. This is the Jesus who had been crucified. This is the Jesus, whose bloodied, dead body had been taken from the cross, wrapped in linen, and entombed by loved followers, the tomb sealed with a large stone, and then carefully guarded by possibly as many as eight Roman soldiers. This is the Jesus who three days later has been resurrected from the dead. The tomb was open and empty. Don't let the familiarity of the resurrection dull the impact and importance of answering the question of who is speaking. The disciples had scattered in fear of their lives at the crucifixion. They were confused and disillusioned at the death of their leader to whom they had devoted three years of their lives following – these same men were now listening to Jesus speak again. Put yourself in the disciples' sandals. If you heard a previously dead man speak to you, I guarantee your mind wouldn't be wandering. You'd be laser focused on each word.

Let's not overlook another question – "Who is the audience?" Look at verses 16-17. They tell us the answer – the original audience is the eleven disciples. These were the eleven men (remember, Judas Iscariot was no longer with them as Matthew 27:3-6 records) that Jesus had specifically chosen to be His closest followers.

1. Simon Peter also called Cephas
2. Andrew (Peter's brother)
3. James (son of Zebedee)
4. John (the son of Zebedee and James' brother)
5. Philip (of Bethsaida)
6. Bartholomew (also known as Nathanael of Cana)
7. Thomas (the twin)
8. Matthew (or known as Levi, the tax collector)
9. James (the son of Alphaeus)
10. Judas (the son of James – not Judas Iscariot also called Thaddaeus)
11. Simon (the zealot)[2]

When we think of this group of eleven, we can easily fall into the trap of thinking of them as super-saints. But these were ordinary men of no special pedigree; men who had normal occupations; men with no formal education; men with families that were as crazy and dysfunctional as most. These everyday eleven had only one extraordinary thing about them. They had all responded to Jesus' call and spent the last three years following Him.

Matthew 4:18-22 records the moment when Jesus called four of them (Simon who is called Peter, his brother Andrew, and James and John, the sons of Zebedee). Jesus issued the clear invitation saying, "Follow me, and I will make you fishers of men." As you read this passage note specifically the response of these men to the invitation.

> *Take a few moments to read this passage and discuss what you might have been thinking or feeling if you were one of these four men. (Record your thoughts here.)*

All eleven of these disciples followed Jesus during His earthly ministry. They followed, not knowing exactly where He was leading them. They followed without fully understanding how long this journey would take. They followed in the joy, excitement and acclaim that came with Jesus, the miracle worker. They were with him side-by-side as they walked the fertile hills of Galilee and listened as He taught. They followed, at first, unsure of the real purpose of what they were signing up for. And they followed Christ to Jerusalem, knowing yet not comprehending that death swirled around their leader. But the most important thing we need to grasp is this– they followed Jesus. And this simple act of faithful obedience to follow is still needed today of every disciple.

Francis Chan writes of the importance of following as a disciple,

> "The word *disciple* refers to a student or apprentice. Disciples in Jesus's day would follow their rabbi (which means teacher) wherever he went, learning from the rabbi's teaching and being trained to do as the rabbi did. Basically, a disciple is a follower, but only if we take the term follower literally. Becoming a disciple of Jesus is as simple as obeying His call to follow."[3]

Following requires a faithful response to move along in the same direction. Followers don't wander off in a hundred other paths of their own choosing. Followers move in cadence with their leader. Following assumes obedience. When a directive is given, a directive is followed. Obedience that is faithful, quick, full. And following also demands imitating. The follower is listening, learning, watching and becoming like his disciple-maker. The Apostle Paul condensed this modeling component of discipleship in 1 Corinthians 11:1 writing, "Be imitators of me, as I am of Christ." (ESV) A follower imitates. Quoting Chan,

> "It's impossible to be a disciple or a follower of someone and not end up like that person…that's the whole point of being a disciple of Jesus: we imitate Him, carry on His ministry and become like Him in the process."[4]

One of the primary objectives in discipleship is to model our lives after Jesus. He is our standard. Through the upcoming weeks as you meet together, your focus will be to become more and more Christ-like.

Let's get back to another question from Matthew 28:18-20. "What does the risen Jesus first say to the eleven followers?" Jesus starts by establishing the extent of His authority. Do you observe the clues that point to the vast extent of His authority? "All", "in heaven and on earth", and "given to Me" all point to the total authority Jesus has. There isn't a smidgen of authority that Jesus lacks – he has it "all." There isn't a square millimeter in all of the heavens or on the earth which is outside His full control. And Jesus is now in full possession of all authority over all things. He is the recipient of the grand master key to the entire kingdom.

Look up these other passages that amplify the extent of Jesus's authority. After reading each of these, provide a few reflections on the overall implications of the extent of Jesus's authority, especially as it relates to the command to make disciples. Write the key words or phrases that jump out to you from each passage, meditate on these, then record the implications.

- Ephesians 1:18-23
- Colossians 1: 15-20
- Colossians 2: 6-10

Implications:

The Risen Savior and Sovereign Lord over both heaven and earth is speaking to those who have followed Him. All of this leads us to our next big question. "What does Jesus command?"

The main verb (action) and object (describes the action) of Jesus' words are short and sweet: "make disciples." This is the clear command. Mark it. Highlight it. Memorize it. But most importantly – OBEY IT! This command is not optional. If we are to be true followers, then we must, Must, MUST respond in faithful obedience to this command issued clearly by our Supreme Commander.

Let's pause right here to have a transparent discussion. The reality is that this clear command has been undervalued and overlooked. We, the church, and so many individually have so soft-sold this command it's been parodied as "The Great Omission" rather than "The Great Commission." When it comes to making disciples, we've dismissed it, generalized it, and spiritualized it to such a degree that nothing much is produced. Or we think it's the job of the church leaders or those with the gift of evangelism like the late Billy Graham. So we leave making disciples up to the "experts." Note Jesus did not leave the job of making disciples to the experts – the Pharisees, High Priests and ruling council. He entrusted the gift of the gospel into the calloused hands of fishermen, tax collectors and other everyday ordinary people.

Corporately as the church and personally as a believer in Christ, why has this command been practically ignored for so long by so many? In other words, what rationale or excuses would we offer on why making disciples has not been a priority?

Corporately

Personally

Let's also pause right here to offer encouragement. The fact that you are now reading this book indicates that you are taking this command to "make disciples" seriously. Meeting together, disciple-maker to disciple, shows that you are now laying aside past excuses to obey. You are reprioritizing, committing to work through these pages together to be a disciple ("be one") and make a disciple ("make one") indicates obedience and verifies that you are truly being a follower of Jesus. Good for you!

Better yet, great for you!!! Followers don't just talk about being a disciple and making a disciple, then hypocritically ignore the command. True followers obey the command and actually do it.

There are two other main questions we want to answer from this passage before we wrap up this first chapter "who?" and "how?" The who question is answered by the description of "all nations." Jesus directs the original eleven to make disciples of all nations. This was certainly a bit of a mind-blow to the eleven Hebrew disciples. Their paradigm held that the nation of Israel was God's chosen people group. But now, the King of Kings was telling His men that disciples would now spread beyond the borders of Israel to all nations, to all people groups.

> *This command to take discipleship to all nations was amplified by Jesus right before his ascension. Read about this in Acts 1: 6-11. In what ways does the command to take discipleship beyond pre-conceived borders impact how you view the command to "make disciples of all nations?" Like expanding concentric circles, taking the gospel to Jerusalem, Judea and Samaria is challenging. Record the personal challenges of such a command. What uncomfortable borders might you have to cross in order to make disciples?*

The "how" question of discipleship is answered by Jesus in two specific ways: baptizing and teaching. Baptism was, and still is, a key component to following Jesus. Baptism is an outward public declaration of an inward change and is another critical step of faithful obedience to our Lord and Savior. We will cover baptism in more detail later in our Deeper Walk series, but for now simply realize that baptism identifies us as a true follower of Christ. We are declaring to the world that we are His.

Teaching is the second "how." The eleven disciples were told to teach "all that I have commanded you." The original disciples had sat under the teaching of Jesus for three years. What an education! It was now time for the students to become the teachers. Never will the learning curve be so elevated as when you transition from student to teacher. This is why the command to "make disciples" is so effective. When the student transitions to the teacher, there is an increased level of responsibility and duty. More is demanded and expected from the teacher. The warning of James 3:1 should perk our ears – "Not many of you should become teachers, my brothers, for you know that we who teach will be judged with greater strictness." (ESV) The disciple now turned disciple-maker must take this teaching role with the utmost care. It is no low bar. But the student-to-teacher process is embedded within discipleship. It simply must take place. It did for the eleven and it must happen for you too! Don't let the thought of being a teacher frighten you away. Being a disciple-maker/teacher doesn't mean you need to know every answer to any question. As questions are asked, enjoy the learning process as you (disciple-maker and disciple) discover the answer together.

How does the thought of being a teacher strike you? What major obstacles would need to be crossed for this to be accomplished?

The discipleship challenge is no slight task. The command to make disciples is daunting. To be like Jesus and to teach His commands is no small order. We can easily feel overwhelmed and inadequate. And these same feelings and thoughts must have been percolating for the eleven who first heard the clear command. That's why the closing assurance by Jesus is so important.

"And behold, I am with you always, to the end of the age."

To "behold" signifies to fix your eyes upon; to see with attention; to observe with care; to direct or fix the mind. What Jesus is about to say is super-important. If you are a bible marker, you must underline or highlight "I am with you always." What a promise! What a difference it would make to fully grasp the significance of those five words.

Read these other "I am with you always" promises and describe the difference it would make in the areas noted. These "I am with you always" statements were specific to each individual, but each reinforces the underlying principle that our God is forever present and forever faithful.

Genesis 28:15

Joshua 1: 6-9

Isaiah 41:10-11

- *Fear* I will not leave you
- *Insecurity* Be strong but follow the law
- *Inadequacy*
  Fear not, I am with you

Can you think of other personal implications of trusting that Jesus is "with you always?"

"Make disciples." This is the clear command given to followers by the One who possesses total authority. And the same Lord who commands is the same One who promises to always be right there with us at every step of our deeper walk of discipleship! As a follower of Christ who is walking in faithful obedience to the clear command to make disciples, you will never have to go it alone (nor should you!). You will never be abandoned.

As you embark down the path to making disciples, tap into the promised presence of Christ. Sense the joy that He has for you as you obey His command. Realize the significance of falling into step with the kingdom-building strategy that He designed and desires to reproduce Christ-like followers. And enjoy the relationship that will develop between disciple and disciple-maker.

"Go. Make disciples." You can do it!

DEEPER WALK QUESTIONS

Discipleship cannot happen in the sterile environment of a classroom. Making disciples is about developing Christ-honoring relationships. Spend time sharing your faith-journey stories with one another. Answer questions like:

- How long have you been a follower of Christ?
  Whole adult life
- When did you first hear the gospel? What was your response?
  My grandparents -
- Did your family attend church growing up? How long have you attended this church?
  Whole life - hated it till I found Highlands
- Where did you grow up and what was it like?
  Grandparents + then Mel & Mom
- Tell me about your family.
  Totally disfunctional

Share your personal expectations of discipleship. What excites you about what is ahead?

Memorize Matthew 28:18-20

Chapter 2

DISCIPLESHIP – An Inspiring Example of Calling

Slightly bent, a slower shuffle, silver haired, but sixty-two years married and still holding hands. You watch closely and they still do the little things to make life easier for the other. He opens the door to help her get in the car. She scrambles his egg just the way he likes it. Simply but significantly – still loving each other. What an example!

Don't you just love to watch those who are doing it right? It might be the slow-mo camera replaying a golf professional's smooth swing, rewinding a YouTube music lesson to see how the musician plays a chord sequence or watching the knife skills of an experienced chef. We can learn so much from those who have excelled in their field. They appear to do so much naturally. But in actuality, like the sixty two year old "newlyweds," it's taken years of practice to make their craft look so easy. But if we watch carefully we can learn from the best.

We are going to take a careful look at Paul and Timothy so we can get a better appreciation of their relationship as disciple maker and disciple. We will see their history together. And from the very opening verse of 2 Timothy, we will understand the importance of knowing who we are (our identity) in Christ and what we are called to do (our calling.)

We want to learn how to "make disciples" from one who did it well – the Apostle Paul. No follower of Christ has made a larger impact on the world stage and for the kingdom of God than Paul. Chuck Swindoll writes,

> "From his obscure birth in Tarsus of Cilicia, through his remarkable conversion en route to Damascus, and along all those journeys from Antioch of Syria to the very presence of Nero enthroned in Rome, including his brutal martyrdom beside the Ostian Way, the man leaves his mark on all who take the time to pause and ponder. Left in the wake of its significance, you're unable to remain the same. A life like Paul's translates into a model anyone would want to emulate. All who examine the Christlikeness woven through the fabric of his character are enriched."[5]

Paul's wake of significance was due, in large part, to his excellence in making disciples. And while we don't have a YouTube to watch, we do have the clarity of the scriptures Paul wrote to observe what he did and how he excelled in discipleship. But before we start to replay Paul's example from scripture, let's do a quick review of what we learned from our first lesson on discipleship.

From Matthew 28:18-20 we are given the clear command to "go and make disciples."

> 18And Jesus came and said to them, "All authority in heaven and on earth has been given to me. 19Go therefore and make disciples of all nations, baptizing them in the name of the Father and of the Son and of the Holy Spirit, teaching them to observe all that I have commanded you. 20And behold, I am with you always, to the end of the age."
>
> Matthew 28: 18-20 ESV

We learned that the goal of disciple-making was directed to followers of Christ. Christ followers are those who align their life to the Absolute Sovereign King. Through their obedience to His teachings, they are being transformed into the image of the One they follow. Specifically, we observed that Jesus stressed baptism (publically identifying ones faith in Christ) and teaching that is based on His commands. And daunting as the challenge of making disciples might be, we were assured that Jesus will always be with us through the process.

Let's get some terminology nailed down. Jesus says to "make disciples." The Greek word used here for the word disciple is mathëteuö (mah thay tyu o). It occurs four times in the New Testament (three times in Matthew and once in Acts. Matthew 28:19, Acts 14:21). From this usage we see that the word disciple has two uses. First, "disciple" is used to identify a follower; one who follows another's precepts and instructions.

> When it was evening, there came a rich man from Arimathea, named Joseph, who also was a disciple of Jesus.
>
> Matthew 27:57 ESV

Secondly, "disciple" can also carry with it the action of teaching, training or instructing.

> And he said to them, "Therefore every scribe who has been trained for the kingdom of heaven is like a master of a house, who brings out of his treasure what is new and what is old."
>
> Matthew 13:52 ESV

The New American Standard Bible renders this verse,

> And Jesus said to them, "Therefore every scribe who has become a disciple of the kingdom of heaven is like a head of a household, who brings out of his treasure things new and old.

So, "disciple" can refer to a person following after another's teaching and to the act of teaching itself.

Taking into account those two uses of the word disciple as shown in scripture, and understanding how both Jesus and Paul discipled others let's consider the term discipleship. Stated as simply as possible, here is our working definition:

"Intentionally multiplying Christ-like followers."

Discipleship is an intentional activity and goal. We don't haphazardly fall into it. We have to keep it clearly before us in attitude and in execution. Secondly, the process of discipleship is about the power of multiplication. Discipleship was the original multi-level marketing strategy. Much more productive than simple addition, when we are correctly implementing discipleship, we will witness the compounding growth of multiplication as two becomes four, four to eight, eight to sixteen, sixteen to thirty-two, and so on. The power of multiplication through disciple making is how God builds His kingdom. And Jesus is our focus and our model. "Follow me as I follow Christ" was Paul's battle cry. And "Christ-like" is our goal. We strive to become more and more like Christ in all we do. And what happens as a result? We become "followers". As we are involved in the discipleship process we will discover the fulfilling reward of following Christ and then seeing our lives, and the lives of those we then disciple, changed in dramatic ways. And there's nothing more significant and joyfully satisfying than playing a small part in that worthy outcome! Discipleship is simply and significantly "intentionally multiplying Christ-like followers."

With definitions established, let's look at the inspiring example of discipleship that Paul provides. If you don't know that much about Paul, his background is an incredible example of the grace of God and the transformational power of Christ.

To know Paul, the world-changing Apostle, we need to first know Saul – the vicious opponent of Christianity. We pick up the prelude to Saul/

Paul's story in Acts 6-7. Here are some excerpts (but it would be more beneficial if you took the time to read the entire chapters.)

> 7And the word of God continued to increase, and the number of the disciples multiplied greatly in Jerusalem, and a great many of the priests became obedient to the faith. 8And Stephen, full of grace and power, was doing great wonders and signs among the people.
>
> Acts 6:7-8 ESV

Stephen is arrested on false charges and stands before the council to answer the charges. Acts 6:15 says Stephen's face was "like the face of an angel". Stephen proceeds to retell the history of Israel beginning with Abraham through Moses, and ends by saying,

> 51You stiff-necked people, uncircumcised in heart and ears, you always resist the Holy Spirit. As your fathers did, so do you. 52Which of the prophets did your fathers not persecute? And they killed those who announced beforehand the coming of the Righteous One, whom you have now betrayed and murdered, 53you who received the law as delivered by angels and did not keep it.
>
> Acts 7:51-53 ESV

Now you can imagine how well that went over. In their eyes what Stephen said amounted to blasphemy. So they stoned him and we have Christianity's first martyr. But look what the very next verses record.

> 1And Saul approved of his execution. And there arose on that day a great persecution against the church in Jerusalem, and they were all scattered throughout the regions of Judea and Samaria, except the apostles. 2Devout men buried Stephen and made great lamentation over him. 3But Saul was ravaging the church, and entering house after house, he dragged off men and women and committed them to prison.
>
> Acts 8:1-3 ESV

In this early stage of the Christian faith Saul is the one leading the opposing attack. And, after his conversion, Paul (renamed from Saul in Acts 13:9) recounts his former days.

Read these passages and give your own description of what kind of character Paul used to be.

- *Acts 22:4-5*
- *Acts 26:9-10*
- *Galatians 1:13-14*

Before Christ, I would describe Paul as ....

But God has His eye on Paul. As only God can do, He pours His mercy and grace into this "foremost of sinners" and Paul is converted. Augustine called Paul's conversion "the violent capture of a rebel will."[6] He pictured it as being like changing the nature of a wild wolf into the spirit of a lamb.

Read about Paul's conversion experience in Acts 9:1-19.

Notice the special pre-planned purpose that God has for Paul.

> 15But the Lord said to him, "Go, for he is a chosen instrument of mine to carry my name before the Gentiles and kings and the children of Israel. 16For I will show him how much he must suffer for the sake of my name."
>
> Acts 9:15-16 ESV

Keep this conversion experience and special purpose tucked away in your memory bank. In the disciple journey ahead you will find an amazing similarity to what God has planned for *you*!

Pause here and spend a little time discussing your past (your "before Christ" days). How would you have described yourself?

Paul spends three obscure years in Arabia (see Galatians 1:11-24) returns to Jerusalem where he is accepted by the Apostle Peter. He then returns to his home in Tarsus for some five, six or more silent years of waiting before being recruited into service by Barnabas. And from that time, Paul will travel throughout the Mediterranean area on three separate missionary journeys. And in the middle of these trips, he encounters Timothy – one of his disciples.

BACKGROUND ON TIMOTHY

We are first introduced to Timothy in Acts 16 during Paul's second missionary journey. He is already a believer at this time, so there is a good chance that Timothy came to faith on Paul's first missionary visit (recorded in Acts 14:8-23).

Read Acts 16: 1-5 and let's test your observation skills. Can you pull out 7 observations about Timothy from this passage?

1.

2.

3.

4.

5.

6.

7.

Timothy accompanies Paul and so starts a mutual ministry that will last for over 15 years. Paul trusts Timothy to the greatest degree- sending him to Corinth as a messenger for Paul and leaving Timothy in Ephesus to protect the integrity of the gospel in this very special church (Paul spent more time in Ephesus than in any other church location – See 1 Corinthians 4:17 and 1 Timothy 1:1-3).

We can observe the special relationship between Paul and Timothy in Philippians 2: 19-22.

> 19I hope in the Lord Jesus to send Timothy to you soon, so that I too may be cheered by news of you. 20For I have no one like him, who will be genuinely concerned for your welfare. 21For they all seek their own interests, not those of Jesus Christ. 22But you know Timothy's proven worth, how as a son with a father he has served with me in the gospel.
>
> Philippians 2:19-22 ESV

From this passage, summarize how Paul would have described Timothy's character?

From this point in our discipleship journey we are going to be focusing our attention on the first two chapters of 2 Timothy. So, as we did with Paul and Timothy, let's get a little historical background on this special letter.

Paul is writing to Timothy who is pastoring the church in Ephesus. Most historians date this letter somewhere around 64-67 AD. This was a time of great unrest within the Roman Empire. On July 18 of 64 AD, a fierce fire swept through Rome. Starting in the Circus Maximus, this fire completely destroyed more than half of the city and burned for over five days. Speculation swirled over the originating source or cause of the fire and many fingers pointed to Emperor Nero. He subsequently pointed the finger of blame to the followers of the Way - (the description of early Christians). And from this point, persecution of Christian believers escalated to a gruesome degree.

Eusebius, a Roman historian of that time, records that Christians were arrested and subjected to various means of unusual torture. They were wrapped in animal skins and put into the great arena with lions. Nero crucified many and used their burning bodies as torches to light his street.

Paul, who approximately two years earlier had been set free from a previous imprisonment was re-arrested. In stark contrast to his prior house arrest, this arrest found him deep in the filthy bowels of the Roman prison system experiencing the worst of conditions.

Under these conditions, Paul writes this letter, his last, to his disciple Timothy. Second Timothy is a deeply personal letter, especially when we recognize that these will be Paul's final words.

Tradition tells us that Paul was executed by beheading just outside of the city on the Ostian Way. But before he meets his executioner, he provides Timothy and the church an extremely useful letter about how to persevere in ministry, especially in the face of suffering. And this last letter from Paul is also an excellent record and an inspiring example of how Paul discipled others.

Paul opens his personal letter thus,

> 1 Paul, an apostle of Christ Jesus by the will of God according to the promise of the life that is in Christ Jesus
>
> 2 Timothy 1:1 ESV

From this one sentence we glean much information. Paul not only identifies himself as the author of the letter, he also declares his personal identity. Then he proceeds to tell of his calling, both wrapped up in a secure promise from Christ. Let's look at each of these components.

EFFECTIVE DISCIPLESHIP STARTS WITH A DIVINE IDENTITY

Like most of his letters, Paul opens by identifying himself as the writer and as "an apostle of Christ Jesus by the will of God." Observe how Paul viewed his identity in these other letters.

> 1 Paul, a servant of Christ Jesus, called to be an apostle, set apart for the gospel of God
>
> Romans 1:1 ESV

[1]Paul, called by the will of God to be an apostle of Christ Jesus,
and our brother Sosthenes,

1 Corinthians 1:1 ESV

[1]Paul, an apostle of Christ Jesus by the will of God, and Timothy our brother

2 Corinthians 1:1a ESV

[1]Paul, an apostle—not from men nor through man, but through Jesus Christ and God the Father, who raised him from the dead—
[2]and all the brothers who are with me

Galatians 1:1-2 ESV

[1]Paul, an apostle of Christ Jesus by the will of God

Ephesians 1:1a ESV

[1]Paul and Timothy, servants of Christ Jesus

Philippians 1:1a ESV

[1]Paul, an apostle of Christ Jesus by the will of God, and Timothy our brother

Colossians 1:1 ESV

[1]Paul, an apostle of Christ Jesus by command of God our Savior and of Christ Jesus our hope,
[2]To Timothy, my true child in the faith

1 Timothy 1:1-2a ESV

Now underline and count all the repeated phrases. What do you observe?

One sure thing about Paul – he didn't have an identity crisis. He knew his divine identity – he knew who he was and whose he was. He knew beyond a shadow of a doubt that his identity was derived from God. This is something we too need for effective discipleship. We need to know our divine identity (who we are in Christ). We will be covering this topic more in depth in a future study, but for now recognize that Paul clearly understood that all that he is and all that he does rests solely on the righteousness of Jesus whose sacrifice on the cross reconciled fallen man to the holy God.

EFFECTIVE DISCIPLESHIP CONSISTS OF A DIVINE CALLING

What is a calling? Unfortunately, most believers think that a "calling" is reserved for those mythical super-saints that retreat to monasteries, work full-time in church or devote themselves to mission work in a foreign country. But calling is something much more common than this exclusive concept. A calling is simply the recognition of a divine summons to follow divine orders with divine empowerment, all according to a divine design. And all believers have been provided a divine summons with divine orders. We all have been divinely summoned by God. It might not (okay probably won't) be as dramatic as the Apostle Paul being blinded and supernaturally healed with a direct vision of the resurrected Lord. But the Lord has sent out a directive and he wants us to respond accordingly. Paul was called to be an apostle to the Gentiles – to share the gospel, disciple, and plant churches through Asia Minor. And not unlike Paul, our goal of discipleship is really nothing more than a step of obedience to the command of Jesus. "Go therefore and make disciples of all nations..." This is our diving calling. Simple. Significant.

Let's look at some other writings of Paul which reinforce how these components work together. When Paul penned his letter to the Colossians, he spoke to his God-appointed calling and purpose.

> [25]of which I became a minister according to the stewardship from God that was given to me for you, to make the word of God fully known, [26] the mystery hidden for ages and generations but now revealed to his saints. [27]To them God chose to make known how great among the Gentiles are the riches of the glory of this mystery, which is Christ in you, the hope of glory. [28]Him we proclaim, warning everyone and teaching everyone with all wisdom, that we may present everyone mature in Christ. [29]For this I toil, struggling with all his energy that he powerfully works within me.
>
> Colossians 1:25-29 ESV

Do these words to the Colossians remind you of the second part of our definition of calling - "to follow divine orders with divine empowerment"?

And we have the same power source as Paul did to accomplish these divine orders – the promised presence of the Holy Spirit. Discipleship is the recognition of our divine summons to intentionally multiply Christ-like followers; it's the step of obedience to follow the direct order to "make disciples"; and it's the daily dependence for God's empowerment to accomplish this significant task. Discipleship is God's design. He crafted this faith-building, kingdom-multiplying strategy to build up His body – and it works!

Paul recognized his divine summons (I became a minister). He was following divine orders (to make the word of God fully known). And third, he was doing so under divine empowerment (with all his energy that he powerfully works within me). He was plugged into the unlimited power source of God's Holy Spirit.

As we embark on the deeper walk of discipleship it is important to embrace the same confidence and purpose that Paul demonstrated to Timothy: to make the word of God fully known and that we may present everyone mature in Christ. Disciple-maker and disciple alike are each called. And, just like Paul, we've been given specific orders on what we should be doing – and that is "make disciples."

What does a greater understanding and appreciation for your calling to make disciples do for you? Record your thoughts here.

The second half of 2 Timothy 1:1 provides another inspiring example from Paul – it is "according to the promise of the life that is in Christ Jesus."

EFFECTIVE DISCIPLESHIP RELIES ON A SECURE PROMISE

Let's look at 2 Timothy 1:1 again paying close attention to the last portion of the verse.

[1]Paul, an apostle of Christ Jesus by the will of God *according to the promise of the life that is in Christ Jesus*

2 Timothy 1:1 ESV (emphasis mine)

Let's not rush right over this phrase "the promise of the life". Exactly what is this? Pay special attention to the seemingly insignificant word "the" which proceeds "life." "The" is a definite article indicating that there is one unique life that Paul has in mind. The verses below help us identify /define what is meant by life. In the first two verses, Jesus is the speaker. In the last one, the apostle John is the speaker.

24 Truly, truly, I say to you, whoever hears my word and believes him who sent me has eternal life. He does not come into judgment, but has passed from death to life.

John 5:24 ESV

40 For this is the will of my Father, that everyone who looks on the Son and believes in him should have eternal life, and I will raise him up on the last day."

John 6:40 ESV

12 Whoever has the Son has life; whoever does not have the Son of God does not have life.

1 John 5:12 ESV

When you respond in faith, you have the secure promise of eternal life and you will pass from death into eternal life. The secure promise of eternal life in heaven is certainly a worthy result of what Jesus did for us. But the promise of life goes beyond eternal life in the future. The promise of life also includes an abundant life now.

10 The thief comes only to steal and kill and destroy. I came that they may have life and have it abundantly.

John 10:10 ESV

Could it be that one of the reasons why so few Christians are failing to experience this abundant life is that we are failing to walk worthy of our calling? We have lost sight of the fulfillment and blessing that God provides when we simply do life as He has prescribed.

We, as followers of Christ, have been given the secure promise of life. But in order to be effective as a disciple maker, we must also realize and take advantage of this secure promise that Jesus provides. It is so important to know, to *really* know our secure position in Christ.

EFFECTIVE DISCIPLESHIP RELIES ON A SECURE POSITION

It is our position in Christ that provides the security, assurance and empowerment that we need and that can free us from so much negative baggage that we foolishly and needlessly carry.

Read the following passages and record the significance of what each has to say about who we are "in Christ".

- *2 Corinthians 5:17*

- *Romans 8:1*

In 2 Timothy, Paul leaves us an inspiring example of what discipleship looks like. And from the opening verse we see that effective disciple makers are clear in their identity and purpose; and they also rely on the secure promise and special position of being in Christ.

DEEPER WALK QUESTIONS

Rephrase or expand on each part of our definition of discipleship describing why it's important.

- Intentionally

- Multiplying

- Christ-like

- Followers

Being completely honest and transparent, how confident are you (1-10 scale) of your "calling"? Which part of our definition of calling gives you the most trouble? Explain your response.

- A Divine Summons
- To Follow Divine Orders
- By Divine Enablement
- According to Divine Design

Our identity as followers of Christ is so critical to everything about our faith walk. Read Ephesians 1: 1-14 and pay special attention to each of the "in Christ" or "in Jesus" references. Write down each of the benefits associated with the phrases "in Christ" or "in Jesus". What are some of the ramifications of such a position? How could this position make a difference in how we relate to others (like our spouse, children or co-workers)?

Chapter 3

DISCIPLESHIP - A Recipe for Relationships

Nestled safe and secured deep within the six-foot high and inches thick stainless steel walls in Atlanta Georgia lies the world's most famous guarded recipe. Ever since Asa Candler purchased the rights to this secret formula in 1891, the ingredients of Coca-Cola have been held in strictest secrecy. It is reported that only two employees are privy to the complete formula at any one time and that these employees are prohibited from ever traveling together (in case they were both killed). When one person dies, the other must choose the next successor and pass the secret on to this trusted employee.

Colonel Harland Sanders used his secret original recipe of eleven herbs and spices to create the Kentucky Fried Chicken empire. Eighteen thousand franchises later, this secret recipe is still producing enough demand to finish off about 800 million chickens per year.

Needless to say, there is power and a whole lot of money that is tied up in a special recipe. But there is another recipe that can be worth a whole lot more than Coca-Cola or KFC. It's the recipe for a healthy relationship. Use the ingredients of this recipe in correct measure and you'll experience the rich, satisfying and long-lasting flavor of a close friend.

But the good part about this recipe is, it's no secret. As Paul starts his last letter to Timothy, anyone can observe six ingredients of this recipe. And, when incorporated into the discipleship process these six ingredients will produce something so tasty "your tongue will slap your brains out."

> [2]To Timothy, my beloved child: Grace, mercy, and peace from God the Father and
> Christ Jesus our Lord. [3]I thank God whom I serve, as did my ancestors, with a
> clear conscience, as I remember you constantly in my prayers night and day. [4]As I
> remember your tears, I long to see you, that I may be filled with joy. [5]I am reminded
> of your sincere faith, a faith that dwelt first in your grandmother Lois and your
> mother Eunice and now, I am sure, dwells in you as well. [6]For this reason I remind
> you to fan into flame the gift of God, which is in you through the laying on of my
> hands, [7]for God gave us a spirit not of fear but of power and love and self-control.
>
> 2 Timothy 1:2-7 ESV

INGREDIENT #1 - HEARTFELT COMMUNICATION

The first ingredient we see from Paul is the heartfelt communication that he shared. "To Timothy, my beloved child". Can you imagine the thoughts and emotions that flowed through Timothy as he read these words? It's been said that every child longs to hear with unwavering certainty the answer to this question: "Do I have what it takes?" As Timothy reads that Paul calls him his "beloved child" there can be no doubt that Paul has a deep affection and appreciation for Timothy – and he isn't reluctant to communicate it.

"Beloved" is the adjective that Paul uses. The Greek word is *agapētos* (ah ga pay tas). It is derived from the root word *agape*. It means dear, esteemed, favorite, worthy of love. The Father used this same word to describe the measure of His love for the Son.

> [16]And when Jesus was baptized, immediately he went up from the water, and behold, the heavens were opened to him, and he saw the Spirit of God descending like a dove and coming to rest on him; [17]and behold, a voice from heaven said, "This is my *beloved* Son, with whom I am well pleased."
>
> Matthew 3:16-17 ESV (emphasis mine)

It seems like heartfelt communication is a fading commodity. Instead of using such relationally deep words like "beloved" we simply attach an emoji. Perhaps we could learn from letters of yesteryear that drip with words of affirmation and appreciation. Consider the following examples from the Civil War:

> How happy the thought that years increase the affection and esteem we have for each other to love and be loved. May it ever be so and may I ever be a husband worthy of your warmest affections.
>
> Attributed to Harvey Black, Brady Station Virginia[7]

> Give my love to the old lady and all the friends. My love and a thousand kisses to my sweet Amanda and our little boys. How my heart yearns for thou that are so near and dear to me. Goodbye my own sweet wife, for the present.
>
> Attributed to J.C. Morris, Lanjer Arkansas[8]

And here's another example of heartfelt communication from a more recent time:

> Dear Mrs. Reagan
>
> There are no words to describe the happiness you have brought to the Gov. It is no secret that he is the most married man in the world and would be totally lost and desolate without you. It seemed to me that you should know this and be aware of how essential you are in the man's life. By his own admission, he is completely in love with you and happier than a Gov deserves. With love and appreciation.
>
> Your in luv Gov.
> (Ronald Reagan to Nancy) [9]

If you want to lay a foundation for those you will disciple, don't hold back on worthy affirmation, encouragement and heartfelt communication! How sad the souls who are left to wonder if they are loved; sadder still the souls of those who fail to express their love to others.

Heartfelt communication like this takes time – time to think and time to share. It also requires a sincere effort. You've got to mean it and express it. And you've got to be vulnerable to share it. There's a bit of risk in this level of communication. But with risk comes reward – and the payback from heartfelt communication is substantial!

INGREDIENT #2 - COMMITMENT TO PRAY

The second ingredient we see that makes the discipleship process so effective and appealing is a commitment to pray. Paul writes, "as I remember you constantly in my prayers night and day." Oh, the power of prayer. Praying for someone is one of the highest honors you can provide for someone else and Paul recognized both the duty and privilege that intercessory prayer offers. And notice that Paul didn't just offer up a one-time quickie prayer. No - he was on his knees continually and repeatedly.

Despite miles and months of separation Paul continued to pray for his disciple, Timothy. Prayers of thanksgiving. Prayers of remembrance. Prayers of supplication. As thoughts of Timothy came to Paul, he repeatedly turned those thoughts into prayers – and what a positive habit to develop!

Nothing changes a relationship more than constant prayer. In addition to praying for someone, pray with them. Your discipleship experience will grow exponentially when you pray with each other. When someone asks for prayer, stop and pray right then and there. You can email your prayers and text them too. I know many women who have a text group and frequently use technology as a means to request and give prayer. Following up on a prayer request to see how God answers the prayer gives a two-fold benefit. First it demonstrates your care for the other person (accomplishing ingredient #1). Secondly, it serves to strengthen the faith of both of you as you repeatedly see God's faithfulness in response to your prayers. That does not mean those prayers will always be answered in the way you desire, but they will be answered in a way that brings God glory and conforms you to likeness of Christ Jesus.

INGREDIENT #3 - EMOTIONAL CONNECTION

We see a third ingredient of this relational recipe for discipleship in verse four. It is an emotional connection between both men. "As I remember your tears, I long to see you, that I may be filled with joy." It is said that some produce joy when they arrive, others when they leave. For Paul, Timothy brought joy when he arrived.

Paul and Timothy spent years together – according to some timelines perhaps up to fourteen years of mutual ministry. So can you imagine the shared experiences and mutual history they had together. Through both good times and bad, these two men did life – together. And this established an emotional connection between them.

Think of these four P's – Peaks, Pits, Praises, and Prayers when it comes to developing an emotional connection with each other. Over the next period of time in your discipleship walk you'll experience the highs and lows of life and you'll be able to express prayers and praises for all the extremes of life.

This emotional tie is one element that separates true discipleship from the classroom. It's hard to become emotionally entwined with another in the sterile environment of tables and chair and books and curriculum. But as we invest time with each other (away from a mere intellectual pursuit), the extremes of the heart ("tears" and "joy") help pave the way for maximum growth. And remember that this sort of emotional connection does take time. Much like a sporting team develops into a unit through a long season, the emotional connection of discipleship doesn't necessarily come quickly. One coach put it this way: "Team takes time!" As you enter into the discipleship process, be careful to engage your heart as well as your head!

Take some time here to read Acts 20:19-38. This passage drips with emotion. What do you see in this passage that relates to this special ingredient?

INGREDIENT #4 - SINCERE COMPLIMENT

The fourth important ingredient in our recipe of relationship that we observe in this opening paragraph is the sincere compliment that Paul gives Timothy. "I am reminded of your sincere faith." Paul's memory of Timothy triggered a written accommodation for Timothy's inherited and sincere faith. Again we see the power that Paul's words must have brought to Timothy. Someone once said, "Some have thousands of reasons why they cannot do what they want to do, when all they really need is one reason why they can." Paul gave Timothy one reason why Timothy could succeed as a disciple – his sincere faith.

Have you ever experienced the uplifting power of someone who believes in you, when perhaps you didn't even believe in yourself? Maybe your mom slipped a note into your lunchbox encouraging you for that big challenge at school. Or tune into the next Hall of Fame induction ceremony or Emmy Awards show and you'll hear testimony of how a sincere belief and compliment helped move an athlete or actress up the ladder of success. When someone offers a sincere compliment, their persuasions can lead to our own and those words can make all the difference in the world. So in your discipleship relationship if you are a

"Paul" show your "Timothy" how strongly you believe in his or her ability to grow and your desire to see the growth and steadfastness in walking through both the hills and the valleys together. Practice the admonition to encourage one another! You will be amazed how it enriches your relationship. (see 1Thessalonians 5:11.)

Read Proverbs 15:23 and 25:11. How do these word pictures emphasize the worth of a sincere compliment?

INGREDIENT #5 - POSITIVE COMMAND

There is a fifth ingredient of discipleship that is needed, but so seldom provided – a positive command is given. Paul issues this imperative – "fan into flame the gift of God..." We have to admire the authoritative nature of Paul's command. He didn't beat around the bush with suggestions or innuendos. He told Timothy plainly – "stir up, rekindle the embers, fan the flame of, and keep burning" (Amplified Bible).

In the modern Christian world, these kinds of direct commands are seldom uttered. When it comes to issues of faith, we frequently lack the resolve and fortitude that it takes to tell someone what to do. But Paul has the backbone to charge Timothy with a specific task. Paul can talk this way not solely because of his authority as apostle – but especially because of the long-standing relationship that these two men have established.

Advice given before trust is established is seldom swallowed. Surely Timothy recognizes that each command issued by Paul is fully backed up with the currency of trust, respect and loyalty. Paul wouldn't command unless it was in the best interest of his spiritual son.

The longer you are in relationship with a discipleship partner, the more opportunity there will be to practice the fine art of speaking the truth in love. In this passage, Paul is challenging Timothy to be bolder in times of potential conflict. When you are committed to bringing out the best in another, you can say the hard things. But you don't need to say them in a hard way!

> *Look at the advice that Paul offers Timothy later in the letter in 2 Timothy 2:24-25. How does this passage complement the "positive command" ingredient?*

INGREDIENT #6 - A MUTUAL COMPANION

Let's finish our recipe of relationship with the sixth and final ingredient needed for effective discipleship. It is subtly described in verse seven in what we will call – a mutual companion. Paul writes, "For God gave us" with emphasis on "us". Paul didn't push his condemning pointer finger toward Timothy and use "you" when he was encouraging Timothy to be courageous. Paul used the inclusive "we" to make his point. By using "we", Paul was letting Timothy know that they were in this discipleship process together. And both men needed to come to grips with the needed recognition that God was offering power and love and self-control rather than being crippled with a debilitating spirit of fear or timidity.

Billy Graham was quoted as saying, "When a brave man takes a stand, the spines of others are strengthened."[10] Timothy's spine stood taller when he heard from Paul that they were in mutual need of God's empowering presence. So as we grow in the discipleship process, realize that both disciple and disciple-maker are in this together.

Dig deep into Ecclesiastes 4:9-12 and see if you can uncover the benefits of a mutual companion. List what you find – and expand on what these benefits would look like in a healthy relationship.

We need to understand that while we are working our way through these discipleship booklets, we are building the process on relationships. You will hear it repeated throughout the "Deeper Walk" series – "relationship trumps curriculum." There needs to be a healthy balance of both relationship and curriculum throughout the discipleship journey. And in the opening verses of 2 Timothy, we see the emphasis on relationship between Paul and Timothy. May this also be said between you, the disciple and your disciple-maker!

As we continue down the path of discipleship ("Intentionally multiplying Christ-like followers") we will do it best by incorporating all six of these ingredients. And no need to keep it a secret – share this recipe!

- Heartfelt Communication
- Commitment to Pray
- Emotional Connection
- Sincere Compliment
- Positive Command
- Mutual Companion

DEEPER WALK QUESTIONS

Can you recall someone expressing a loving affirmation to you? What thoughts or emotions did that affirmation produce? How easy is it for you to communicate (verbally and directly) your love for others?

How easy/difficult is it for you to observe and communicate honorable traits in others? Could you do so already? Take turns and offer a sincere compliment and watch what happens.

How do you do when receiving positive criticism from others? Can you humbly receive it and gracefully give it? What factors make both of these steps easier?

The effective disciple-maker understands the importance of "us". Remember – "As one!" Take a brief moment to share what each of you have personally learned so far.

If you were to analyze the six ingredients mentioned in this chapter, rank them (1-6) in terms of your strength.

- ☐ Heartfelt Communication
- ☐ Commitment to Pray
- ☐ Emotional Connection
- ☐ Sincere Compliment
- ☐ Positive Command
- ☐ Mutual Companion

For the two lowest ranked components what specific action could you take to start improving those aspects of your relationships?

1.

2.

Chapter 4

DISCIPLESHIP - Purpose with the Pain

What do an expectant mother and a Navy Seal recruit have in common? Both know that pain is right around the corner. Expectant moms and Seals both recognize that what they will shortly experience will push their pain tolerance to and beyond their physical and emotional limits. Yet moms continue to scream through delivery and brave men and women still vie for the honor of serving as Navy Seals. Why? Why endure the pain? Because both know that there is incredible reward that will follow the extreme discomfort. There is purpose and payout with the pain.

Here we are only a few weeks into the discipleship journey and we are faced with the reality that what's ahead isn't (or shouldn't be) a comfortable walk in the park. Following Christ is costly. If nothing else, it requires an investment of our most precious assets – our time and heart. And as we will discover, when we re-orient our entire life to God; when we base our convictions, attitudes and actions on Him; when we dedicate our identity and purpose to be a disciple-maker, there will be some amount of suffering. Count on it.

After providing an emotion-filled opening seven verses, Paul turns the corner and issues a sobering reminder that following Christ is a painful journey. But the pain has purpose.

> [8]Therefore do not be ashamed of the testimony about our Lord, nor of me his prisoner, but share in suffering for the gospel by the power of God, [9]who saved us and called us to a holy calling, not because of our works but because of his own purpose and grace, which he gave us in Christ Jesus before the ages began, [10]and which now has been manifested through the appearing of our Savior Christ Jesus, who abolished death and brought life and immortality to light through the gospel, [11]for which I was appointed a preacher and apostle and teacher, [12]which is why I suffer as I do. But I am not ashamed, for I know whom I have believed, and I am convinced that he is able to guard until that day what has been entrusted to me.
>
> 2 Timothy 1:8-12 ESV

In the opening section of 2 Timothy, Paul spells out the probability of pain. He doesn't skirt it. Doesn't sugar-coat it. Doesn't even try to rationalize it. In fact, he invites Timothy to it. That's like inviting someone over for a root canal. Who would accept that kind of invitation? Answer: only someone who saw the over-riding benefit and results of enduring the pain. The potential future gain exceeds the reality of present pain.

Paul is wise in providing this up-front disclosure of the pain of being a Christ-follower. If we fail to understand the reality of pain we can be surprised and caught off guard. That's why the dental assistant tells us "This might sting a little." We can prepare for it more effectively when we know it's coming. Paul is preparing Timothy in the same way. He doesn't want his protégé to be surprised and overwhelmed at the hard road ahead.

Paul's forewarning of suffering is also providing Timothy time to weigh his options and carefully consider what he's up against. With such a preemptive notice, Timothy will have no excuse to say, "This isn't what I signed up for!" It's the same principle behind what Jesus told his disciples when he asked them to count the cost of following him.

25 Now great crowds accompanied him, and he turned and said to them, 26 "If
anyone comes to me and does not hate his own father and mother and wife and
children and brothers and sisters, yes, and even his own life, he cannot be my
disciple. 27 Whoever does not bear his own cross and come after me cannot be
my disciple. 28 For which of you, desiring to build a tower, does not first sit down
and count the cost, whether he has enough to complete it? 29 Otherwise, when he
has laid a foundation and is not able to finish, all who see it begin to mock him, 30
saying, 'This man began to build and was not able to finish.' 31 Or what king, going
out to encounter another king in war, will not sit down first and deliberate whether
he is able with ten thousand to meet him who comes against him with twenty
thousand? 32 And if not, while the other is yet a great way off, he sends a delegation
and asks for terms of peace. 33 So therefore, any one of you who does not renounce
all that he has cannot be my disciple.

Luke 14:25-33 ESV

Discipleship requires suffering and some measure of pain.

Let's add a bit of explanation here. In verse 26, Jesus isn't proposing that we hate our families. He is using hyperbole to point out the dramatic difference that followers of Christ should have between a family-love and a God-love. Our love for God should be so great that the love we have for family would seem like hate in comparison. And in verse 27 – "bearing his own cross" signifies the daily sacrifices that a follower of Christ must bear. Each of these points is emphasizing the principle that following Christ is not an easy proposition.

What do you think this suffering or pain looks like? Can you think of any examples from your personal journey of faith? Record your thoughts here.

For most of us, we are not necessarily talking about physical pain although Paul and others did experience that. In a broader sense we are talking about suffering - the state of undergoing pain, distress, or hardship.

It might be helpful to see suffering in both the Old and New Testament perspectives. In the Old Testament, the Jewish mind dealt with suffering as concrete rather than abstract. So if suffering occurred there must be a cause and a purpose behind it. For example, suffering was considered punishment for sin. (See John 9:1-3.) Suffering of the righteous was a problem. (This is why Job's friends could not understand why Job maintained his innocence.) But suffering, even for the righteous is a tool that God employs for several reasons. First, suffering serves to get people's attention. Someone said that pain is God's megaphone. Secondly, suffering can be used to correct sinful behavior and turn the recipient back to obedience. God's discipline can fit in this category. Thirdly, suffering can also be used by God to develop or refine our character to be more Christ-like.

Take some time to explore the following passages that deal with suffering. Which category of suffering do these passages represent?

- *Psalm 25:15-22*
- *Proverbs 22:3 and 27:12*
- *Lamentations 3: 1-24*

In the New Testament there was a perspective shift for suffering – there is a greater understanding and acceptance of pain and suffering. They witnessed, firsthand, the suffering of Christ on the cross. If Christ suffered, then they would also. They also experienced the suffering that comes with taking a stand against a world system that is diametrically opposed to that of Christ. If the world hated Jesus' message, the world would also hate the Lord's messengers. And the New Testament portrays suffering for Christ's sake as a privilege and an honor.

Here are some New Testament passages which speak to this different perspective of suffering. As above, how would you categorize (or summarize) each passage's perspective on suffering?

- *James 1:2-4*
- *1 Peter 4:12-14*
- *Hebrews 12:5-11*

One thing is certain – suffering is a part of life in a broken world. So going back to Paul's statement to Timothy, what perspective does he provide regarding pain or suffering?

There are four aspects of pain that Paul has in mind. First is the pain of "shame."

PAIN OF SHAME

8Therefore do not be ashamed of the testimony about our Lord, nor of me his prisoner

2 Timothy 2:8a ESV

It's not that Timothy is ashamed, but the temptation is there. Paul is warning Timothy not to be ashamed of the message or the messenger. Pastor John Stott observes,

> Man is tempted to be ashamed of the name of Christ, the people of Christ or the gospel of Christ. "Indeed if this were not a temptation common to man, the Lord Jesus would not have needed to issue the solemn warning, 'For whoever is ashamed of me and of my words in this adulterous and sinful generation, of him will the Son of Man also be ashamed when he comes in the glory of his Father with the holy angels.'" (Mark 8:38)[11]

For believers in Paul's day (and more increasingly in ours), followers of Christ were the minority and were often ostracized by the community. The social, religious and government systems made it extremely difficult to stand in Christ's corner. Indeed, Paul was in prison as a result of his stand for Christianity, and his hope was that Timothy wouldn't feel the pain of shame for either Paul or about standing true to the testimony of faith in Jesus. This pain of shame is closely tied to our fear of rejection. When we are bold to let others know we believe in Christ, we are an open target for ridicule.

Paul was concerned for believers in this area of shame or fear. He wrote in his letter to the Romans similar warnings and instruction.

> 16 For I am not ashamed of the gospel, for it is the power of God for salvation to everyone who believes, to the Jew first and also to the Greek. 17 For in it the righteousness of God is revealed from faith for faith, as it is written, "The righteous shall live by faith."
>
> Romans 1:16-17 ESV

In addition to not being ashamed of the message, Paul asks Timothy not to be ashamed of him, the messenger, who was currently a prisoner in Rome. Paul did not consider himself a prisoner of Rome, but of the Lord. That awareness makes a huge difference in how we analyze the painful circumstances around us.

Following are some additional passages where Paul reframes his "prisoner" status. How could this perspective help you reframe your period of suffering?

[1]For this reason I, Paul, a prisoner for Christ Jesus on behalf of you Gentiles

Ephesians 3:1 ESV

[1]I therefore, a prisoner for the Lord, urge you to walk in a manner worthy of the calling to which you have been called, [2] with all humility and gentleness, with patience, bearing with one another in love, [3] eager to maintain the unity of the Spirit in the bond of peace.

Ephesians 4:1-3 ESV

Paul, a prisoner for Christ Jesus, and Timothy our brother

Philemon 1a ESV

Now we may never experience literal imprisonment in our country, but in what ways might our ability to share the gospel be impinged upon?

PAIN OF SHARED SUFFERING

There is a second major type of pain that Paul has in mind – the pain of "shared suffering." Paul invites Timothy to partner up with him in suffering. It's one thing to suffer alone, it's another to suffer with others. If misery loves company, so does suffering. Paul discloses the reality of shared suffering and in some manner it had to add a small measure of reassurance. When we encounter shared suffering we are able to distribute the load to another and there is a mutual strength gained when we don't isolate ourselves. (See Ecclesiastes 4:9-12) And Paul assures Timothy that the shared suffering is also fortified with the power of God. Suffering drawn from our own reservoir will soon run dry, but not so with divine empowerment. That's a power source that is endless. (If we could only keep tapped into it!)

People will actually buy into shared pain or suffering if they believe enough in the cause for which they are fighting. We see this in times of war. Winston Churchill would call for shared suffering as he implored the British nation in his radio address, "I have nothing to offer but blood, sweat and tears."[12] And because of their love and loyalty for country, the British people rallied to share in the suffering to which Churchill called them. People will also enter into shared suffering if they are devoted to their suffering partner. Athletic teams suffer with each other, based on mutual devotion. So do soldiers in the same platoon or spouses in marriage. Care enough for another and you'll do most anything to support them. So, the key question for us – do we believe in the Gospel enough that we would willingly enter into suffering for it?

And, in case you think that this might have simply been a one-time remark, consider how Paul repeats this shared suffering theme in every chapter of 2 Timothy.

3Share in suffering as a good soldier of Christ Jesus

2 Timothy 2:3 ESV

[10]You, however, have followed my teaching, my conduct, my aim in life, my faith, my patience, my love, my steadfastness, [11]my persecutions and sufferings that happened to me at Antioch, at Iconium, and at Lystra—which persecutions I endured; yet from them all the Lord rescued me. [12]Indeed, all who desire to live a godly life in Christ Jesus will be persecuted, [13]while evil people and impostors will go on from bad to worse, deceiving and being deceived.

2 Timothy 3:10-13 ESV

[5]As for you, always be sober-minded, endure suffering, do the work of an evangelist, fulfill your ministry.

2 Timothy 4:5 ESV

Again, we are not expected to bear this shared suffering alone. This isn't a "buck up and take it like a man (or woman)" exhortation. Paul tells Timothy that we can endure this suffering "by the power of God." (2 Timothy 1:8b)

PAIN OF HOLINESS

There is a third kind of pain that Paul mentions. It is the pain of "holiness".

[9] who saved us and called us to a holy calling, not because of our works but because of his own purpose and grace, which he gave us in Christ Jesus before the ages began, [10] and which now has been manifested through the appearing of our Savior Christ Jesus, who abolished death and brought life and immortality to light through the gospel,

2 Timothy 1:9-10, ESV

The calling that God has issued is a "holy calling". In other words, we are called to stand separate from a sin-polluted world. Agree to a holy calling and you are committing to a lifetime of being distinctly different.

A disciple can no longer play the chameleon and blend in with the crowd. If we choose to follow a holy calling, behavior changes to reveal something radically different from a culture that accepts, approves and applauds all manners of ungodliness.

Holiness is an attribute of God with four distinct meanings. First, it means to be "set apart". This applies to places where God is present, like the Temple and the tabernacle, and to things and persons related to those holy places or to God Himself – think priests, the ark of the covenant, the Holy of Holies. Second, holiness means to be "perfect, transcendent, or spiritually pure, evoking adoration and reverence." This applies primarily to God, but secondarily to saints or godly people. Think of the admiration that Billy Graham received for his godly ministry. Third, it means something or someone who evokes "veneration or awe, being frightening beyond belief." This is clearly the application to God and is the primary meaning of "holy." Finally, holy means "filled with superhuman and potential fatal power." This speaks of God, but also of places or things or persons which have been set apart by God's presence. A saint is a holy person. To be sanctified is to be made holy. When we place our faith in Christ, we are instantly a saint, but the process of sanctification (being made more and more like Christ) lasts a lifetime.

We have been saved and called to a holy life. Holiness means we won't settle or compromise for the cheap substitutes or empty promises of that which is outside of God's design and plan. And dedicating ourselves to a holy life will involve some measure of suffering, because it is painful to be different from yet still live in an unholy world. (See Romans 12:1-2)

Chuck Swindoll provides a healthy perspective of holiness. He writes,

> It's almost as though holiness is the private preserve of an austere group of monks, missionaries, mystics and martyrs. But nothing could be further from the truth. I couldn't be in greater agreement with Chuck Colson's statement in *Loving God:* "Holiness is the everyday business of every Christian. It

evidences itself in the decisions we make and things we do, hour by hour, day by day."[13]

PAIN OF PUBLIC PAIN

There is fourth and final pain. It is subtle from Paul's pen, but important in practice. It is "public" pain. Paul reveals his identity in a three-fold way – as a preacher, apostle and teacher (1 Timothy 1:11). Paul's calling manifests itself in these three related public roles. As a preacher Paul is actively and openly declaring the gospel message of Jesus. As an apostle, Paul has been specifically and divinely chosen to authoritatively declare truth. And as a teacher Paul is passionate about communicating and transferring scriptural principles that strengthen others. These three identities paint a target on Paul. He is a public figure willing to communicate the gospel – and with that purpose and identity comes a linked pain to any who are willing to display their faith to others.

You are certainly not an apostle; chances are great you're not a preacher; but more than likely you are a teacher and certainly you are a Christ follower. And because of this, you, like Paul, are putting your faith on display to others. As a disciple-maker you take on an instructional role. And if you are a mom or dad, "teacher" is part of your job description. And if you aren't ashamed to display your Christianity in the marketplace, you are "teaching" and "preaching" simply by your attitude and conduct. Paul is modeling the courage it takes to take a public stance for our Christian faith.

The pain of shame. The pain of shared suffering. The pain of holiness. The pain of public pain. With these four kinds of pain before Timothy, we couldn't really blame him if he backed off (especially those of us with a low threshold of pain). We could logically understand if he said "no thanks". But Timothy doesn't. And so we must ask ourselves "Why?" Why would Timothy and why would countless disciples after him be willing to endure any one or all four kinds of pain?

The answer is – for the gain of it all.

> [12] which is why I suffer as I do. But I am not ashamed, for I know whom I have believed, and I am convinced that he is able to guard until that day what has been entrusted to me.
>
> 1 Timothy 1:12 ESV

The gain is all wrapped around one very important object – Christ Jesus. Paul doesn't specifically call out Jesus by name. He refers to Jesus as "whom I have believed". In other words, Paul says that all he is asked to endure and suffer is done so based on the person of Jesus Christ. This is quite a statement and it attests to the life-changing power that Paul found in Jesus and testified about in Acts 9. Belief in Jesus provides the perspective to put problems and present suffering in their proper place – under the authority and sovereignty of Christ Jesus, the author and perfecter of our faith. Jesus – the One who sustains all things; the One who sits in a position of sovereign power; the One who knows the smallest details; the One who personally has experienced the pain of earth; the One who conquered death and who will return again - victorious. It is Jesus who provides all the gain that Paul needs to endure the pain.

And Paul doesn't waiver about the gain that comes with belief in Christ. He says "I am convinced that he is able…" The Greek word translated "convinced" speaks to full assurance of mind; it is being fully persuaded by argument or a belief that is confident and trusting. Such confidence allows Paul not only to persevere now – but also to anticipate in the future. Jesus is on ongoing duty to guard what has been entrusted to Paul. In other words, Paul is looking forward to a future reward that will be handled by Jesus Himself. That's some kind of "gain" for sure!

This anticipation of future gain isn't a new thought from Paul's pen. He wrote to the Philippians with the same sense of anticipation for the future and endurance for the present.

[19]for I know that through your prayers and the help of the Spirit of Jesus Christ this
will turn out for my deliverance, [20]as it is my eager expectation and hope that I
will not be at all ashamed, but that with full courage now as always Christ will
be honored in my body, whether by life or by death. [21]For to me to live is Christ,
and to die is gain. [22]If I am to live in the flesh, that means fruitful labor for me. Yet
which I shall choose I cannot tell. [23]I am hard pressed between the two. My desire
is to depart and be with Christ, for that is far better. [24]But to remain in the flesh is
more necessary on your account. [25]Convinced of this, I know that I will remain and
continue with you all, for your progress and joy in the faith, [26]so that in me you may
have ample cause to glory in Christ Jesus, because of my coming to you again.

Philippians 1:19-26 ESV

Present pain is endured much better when we keep the future gain in mind. Perhaps it is this balance of pain/gain that missionary Jim Elliot had in mind when he wrote in his journal, "He is no fool who gives what he cannot keep to gain what he cannot lose."[14]

Are you willing to endure that "pain" of discipleship? You will be if you are convinced of the gain!

Disciples – join hands with expectant mothers and Navy Seals. Get ready for the pain, but look forward for the purpose and gain that will follow.

DEEPER WALK QUESTIONS

The life of discipleship begins with a turning away from our old life. How is this pictured in the following verses?[15]

Galatians 2:20

John 12:24–25

Luke 14:26 [consider Abraham and Isaac]

What things keep us from surrendering to Christ?

THE MARKS OF A DISCIPLE[16]

Disciples had characteristics that identified them with their teacher and his teaching. The followers of Jesus were no exception. Jesus was careful to talk with them about who they were becoming as they developed as

His disciples. These were not things they quickly incorporated into their lives, but characteristics that they developed over a lifetime.

Jesus instructed His followers about the characteristics that would identify them.

John 15:8

John 13:34–35

John 8:31

Luke 14:33

Matthew 6:24

Consider these characteristics. Why are they important for those who follow Christ? Why might Jesus highlight these particular areas?

What degree of "shame" do you carry when sharing your faith? What are some potential causes for why we feel "shame" for our faith or for our personal testimony?

Have you ever been subject to pain or suffering for taking a personal stand for holiness? What happened (either positively or negatively) and what did you learn as a result?

The pain of discipleship and following Jesus isn't meant to be a solo experience. It's to be shared – with others and with God. Is your tendency to be a loner or can you share your pain?

Paul was calling Timothy to be willing to endure public pain. How public is your faith? Where do you stand on the private/public spectrum of your faith?

"Present pain is endured much better when we keep the future gain in mind." It might be a very difficult thing to do – but visualize what your last few hours of life would feel like. What will you be thinking? How would you be answering these reflective questions: "*What kind of person was I? What kind of spouse, parent, friend?" What kind of follower of Christ was I?*" What is the Holy Spirit telling you about this lesson of suffering and the possible response to these questions?

Review Luke 14:25-35. What costs/suffering are i*nvolved in following Jesus as his disciple? Put these principles into today's culture. What might Jesus be asking of you?*

Chapter 5

DISCIPLESHIP - Patterns to Follow

Some of us are pattern followers – you know, the kind that gets a new TV and immediately pulls out the instruction manual and diligently reads every page from front to back. These kind not only read every page – they will faithfully follow along step by step; they will inventory every part before assembly; they will fill out the warranty card (and mail it in too!).

Or there's the kind of person who will get that same TV and immediately plug it in and see how it works. Instruction manual??? Hardly! Who needs that? This person would rather scrape their fingers on a chalkboard than be subject to the fine print and sequential order of an instruction booklet. If they can see the color picture on the front of the box, they've got all the instructions they need. They will do their best to make it look like the front cover. And sure, there will probably be extra parts when done. But after all, doesn't every manufacturer put extra screws, nuts, plates, and other non-essential pieces into a box just to confuse the consumer?

Are you a manual reader or a manual skipper?

Regardless how you answer that question, one thing is common for all of us. We are all influenced by the models we see before us. If you don't believe that, look back to your high school yearbook and notice how so many fell into line dressing and looking like each other. What were we thinking? We were thinking like lemmings and simply followed the models we had before us. And it doesn't stop in high school. We still jump into the current of public opinion. How many homes are now decorated with the color tones set by Chip and Joanna Gaines?

We are all influenced by the models we see.

And so it should not surprise us at all that in the disciple-making process, a model is given to follow. Paul's relationship with Timothy has been the master example that we're observing and investigating. And the next few verses in 2 Timothy provide several other illustrations that show us the how-to and the how-not-to of discipleship. So, even if you are not the detailed type, fight the urge to skip over the "manual" and let's learn from these positive and negative patterns.

Before we look at these patterns let's do a quick review of where we last left off.

The New Living Translation renders 2 Timothy 1:12 this way,

> That is why I am suffering here in prison. But I am not ashamed of it, for I know the one in whom I trust, and I am sure that he is able to guard what I have entrusted to him until the day of his return.

Paul is confident. And his confidence is grounded knowing that his faith is in a living person – Jesus Christ. Paul is sure that Christ will never leave him. He knows without a doubt that the character of God will never change. And Paul is confident that God Himself will preserve the gospel message. Paul had a job to do and is sold out to do it well, but he knows the spread of Christianity doesn't fall only on his or Timothy's shoulders. They are only the messengers. His confidence rests firmly on God.

Now Paul instructs Timothy about the importance of following a trustworthy pattern.

13Follow the pattern of the sound words that you have heard from me, in the faith
and love that are in Christ Jesus. 14By the Holy Spirit who dwells within us, guard
the good deposit entrusted to you. 15You are aware that all who are in Asia turned
away from me, among whom are Phygelus and Hermogenes. 16May the Lord grant
mercy to the household of Onesiphorus, for he often refreshed me and was not
ashamed of my chains, 17but when he arrived in Rome he searched for me earnestly
and found me— 18may the Lord grant him to find mercy from the Lord on that
day!—and you well know all the service he rendered at Ephesus.

2 Timothy 1:13-18 ESV

Paul wastes no time in providing Timothy the theme of this section. "Follow the pattern" is the command given. And it is an interesting word that Paul uses with "pattern". The word in Greek literally means the under sketch. With Paul's vocation as a tent maker we can understand his familiarity with this word picture. He would use an "under sketch" to lay out and cut the material that would be used to build tents. Much like the flimsy paper used by a seamstress, a "pattern" was used to provide a reliable and sure product. Paul was letting Timothy know that the pattern of sound, healthy words that Timothy had heard or read from Paul could be used to build Timothy's own ministry. And these words were laced in truth and doctrine along with faith and love in Christ – what an example to follow. Christ-centered, Christ-like words of truth, doctrine, faith and love.

Let's pretend that you've had a tape recorder that has tracked your words over the last two weeks. If we replayed that recording would it reflect words of truth, faith and love? How would you describe the words that typically come from your mouth?

It takes great courage to be able to point to yourself as the example. But Paul's confidence isn't self-based. Paul's ability to use himself as an example to follow is based on the model that Paul uses for his own life. We read about this model in 1 Corinthians 11:1 (ESV).

1 Be imitators of me, as I am of Christ.

The NIV version renders it this way: "Follow my example, as I follow the example of Christ." Paul uses a different word in this command. The English word "example" is from the Greek word *"mimetes"* (where we get our words mimic or mimeograph). A *mimetes* was an imitator – think of the parrot that mimics his owner's voice. Paul could put himself before Timothy either as a pattern or as an example because Paul was mimicking the life of Jesus. And really, doesn't that take us back to our definition of discipleship – "Intentionally multiplying Christ-like followers." We want to pattern our words, our thoughts, and our deeds after Christ – the ultimate model and example to follow!

What are the "sound words" that Timothy heard from Paul? The word "sound" means healthy, uncorrupt, whole or without error. Those would be some outstanding words. In a world that spews unhealthy speech in such volume that a sailor's profanity hardly seems out of place, healthy words are so needed. In our divisive climate with vitriol attacks from both sides of the aisle, whole and uncorrupt words would be such a welcome change. And with media intent on speaking and printing words to grab headlines and ratings with little regard for their veracity, words without error seem rare. Paul tells Timothy – model your speech after mine.

A second command is given in this modeling example. "Guard the good deposit that was entrusted to you." To "guard" means to keep or protect something of value or importance. An important prisoner was kept under "guard" and protected. A valuable piece of jewelry was locked away and "guarded" for safe-keeping. Paul here is encouraging Timothy to guard, protect and closely watch "the good deposit". Most likely, Paul is referring to the good deposit of the gospel of truth that Timothy had received and that was transferred from Paul to his trustworthy disciple.

Guarding isn't a cavalier activity to be taken lightly. You must be diligent, attentive and vigilant to be a good "guard". Like the experienced fly fisherman who is constantly attentive to the slightest twitch or very light change of pressure on the line, or the new mother who is ever-so-attentive to hear her newborn's cry, so we too are called to be diligent to guard the truth.

We can be a better disciple-maker and follower of Christ if we learn the fine art of being diligent, attentive and vigilant to protect the gospel of truth. And the gospel message of Christianity needs to be guarded, perhaps more than ever. The truth is under attack and needs to be lifted up, held secure and protected. We need to defend it. The truth is now under-appreciated by a world that has discounted truth and traded it for relativism. We need to treasure the truth and bring back the value it once held in our society. The truth is also under-utilized and we need to make sure that we ourselves are using it and helping others use it too. Let's guard this good deposit that we've been given!

Can you get specific on how to guard this good deposit of truth? How could you

- *Defend the truth –*
- *Treasure the truth –*
- *Use the truth –*

Paul next takes a different track and points to two negative examples. This would be like those pictures in the instruction manual that have a big red circle with a line through it and a bold "**NO!**" next to it. The negative examples are two fellows with difficult to pronounce names – Phygelus and Hermogenes. These men are now forever identified as deserters. For unspecified reasons, these two men who once were faithful are now no-where-to-be-seen. This must have caused quite a bit of emotional pain for Paul – enough to call them out by name! Such is the result of unfaithfulness in those we once held close and trusted. If we are to learn a positive principle from these negative examples it could be simply – "be faithful." Rather than be the kind of person who comes and goes, remain steady; be consistent; be reliable; be committed to go the distance even when the going is tough and unpopular. And boy, does the world need that kind of believer today! Ours is a throw-away world; marriages can easily be ended with no-fault divorce; pews are filled with church-hopping consumers and attenders; and promises are easily broken in business, in church and in families. Let's put the circle and diagonal line across this kind of unfaithfulness and say "**NO!**" to being that kind of fair-weather believer.

Paul moves quickly back to the positive kind of model and points out another guy worth following – Onesiphorus. (Another hard name to pronounce!) It's been said before that some people bring joy with their arrival, others with their departure. Onesiphorus was the former. When Paul saw Onesiphorus coming it was like a welcoming cool breeze on a hot and muggy afternoon. He was a positive influence who was persistent ("searched for me earnestly") as well as courageous ("not ashamed").

Wouldn't we love to have more people like that in our world? When we are tired, exhausted and fatigued, the "refreshers" come in and fill our sails with a breeze that can lift our spirits and keep us headed in the right direction. When discouraged, the "refreshers" can say just the right word to turn a gloomy disposition into one of hope and encouragement. If doubt or fear cripples us into complacency or procrastination, it is the "refresher" who gives us the extra measure of fortitude to try or to try again. So wouldn't it make sense if we so want to be around "refreshers" that we'd find incredible value in being one ourselves? What a positive model to follow by being just like Onesiphorus.

There's one final observation we can pull from Onesiphorus – he was a consistent example. ("you know very well in how many ways he helped me...") His example wasn't a flash-in-the-pan, one-time example. Onesiphorus was a constant steady model to follow. You could go back and trace example after example of how this man proved to be a positive model. He did it all the time! He did it in with the home crowd in Ephesus and he did the same thing with Paul in Rome. Whenever and wherever, Onesiphorus was a constant model to follow. Who wouldn't want to be like that kind of person? Not a hypocrite that changed his actions like a chameleon changes colors, but a forever example of consistency, no matter the cost and no matter the environment.

Here's a summary of the kind of model to follow:

- Be an example.
- Be on guard.
- Be faithful.
- Be a positive influence.
- Be consistent.

If we can follow this kind of model, we will be well on the way to becoming a fully assembled, fully functioning follower of Christ. (And there won't be parts left over!)

DEEPER WALK QUESTIONS

Why is it so important to have a pattern to follow? How does it especially help to have Paul's words and the faith and love found in Jesus as a model to follow?

"Deposit" and "entrusted" are used in a positive sense to protect something of great value. Guarding like this takes the diligence provided by the indwelling Holy Spirit. When tempted to deviate from our perfect "pattern," how does the Holy Spirit help us get back on track?

How do you guard the gospel truth?

Sometimes it helps to have a negative example of what NOT to do. As you examine the negative example of desertion by Paul's two former co-ministers, have you ever felt the kind of pain of being deserted? What thoughts or feelings did you encounter? How can this negative example help us to be a positive example?

From the positive model of Onesiphorus we can learn three important principles. For each – write an idea on how you can apply it in your world.

- Be an encouragement.

- Be bold and courageous.

- Be committed.

Take a look at another example of this kind of "refresher" man - read about Epaphroditus in Philippians 2:25-30. You'll see similar kinds of qualities from him too! What positive qualities do you see? Note two that stand out to you and try to be specific on what you could do to model these qualities.

1.

2.

Chapter 6

DISCIPLESHIP - Pass It On

Something happened in the 2008 Olympic Games that had never happened before and made front page headlines. Both the USA's men's and women's 4x100 relay teams were disqualified because they each failed to pass the baton. Despite being hands-down favorites, the speed of the racers didn't matter because the baton hit the ground and the race was over.

As we approach the finish line of our first study on discipleship, this lesson focuses on one key principle - the importance of passing it on.

Let's start by asking a question that you may be too young to start thinking about. *"What do you possess that you want to pass on?"*

The first thing that pops into our minds would probably be those things that are most valuable - the house, jewelry, cars. But we also would want to pass on those things that are the most meaningful - heirlooms that you had received from your parents or grandparents, an old bible with personal notes from your mother, your first rifle, the autographed baseball from Hank Aaron or the banged up steel measuring cup from your great-grandmother.

We pass on those things that are most valuable and most meaningful. And we don't leave those kind of things up for grabs like a free-for-all or tug-of-war. If we are serious about passing down that which means the most, we will be deliberate and thoughtful about each item. "Who would most treasure this item?" would influence each decision.

More than heirlooms or memorable souvenirs we have the ability to pass on something of extreme and eternal value. Each of us who are believers have the privilege and the important responsibility to pass on the baton of faith to the next generation of believers.

Today we reach the crescendo passage in this quest to understand the important components of discipleship. But before the cymbals crash on the crescendo, let's go back to the opening score to hear again the theme of the Great Commission given by Jesus.

> 18 And Jesus came and said to them, "All authority in heaven and on earth has been given to me. 19 Go therefore and make disciples of all nations, baptizing them in the name of the Father and of the Son and of the Holy Spirit, 20 teaching them to observe all that I have commanded you. And behold, I am with you always, to the end of the age.
>
> Matthew 28: 18-20 ESV

Hopefully by now the melody of this key passage has stuck in your heads. We are to be about the business of making disciples. This is our calling. Jesus has asked us to join him in building his kingdom, and his way of expanding isn't in constructing larger church buildings, schools or seminaries or even in hiring more pastors. God's plan was to spread the gospel through ordinary people in relationship with other ordinary people just like them. The way that we can fulfill our calling is to be actively involved in making disciples.

Before we get to the next point, let's reflect and review. What have you learned so far about this process of discipleship? What has stood out?

Matthew 28:18-20 provides the "what" of discipleship. Today we have a clear passage that serves as the foundational "how" of discipleship.

> [1]You then, my son, be strong in the grace that is in Christ Jesus. [2]And the things you have heard me say in the presence of many witnesses entrust to reliable men who will also be qualified to teach others.
>
> 2 Timothy 2:1-2 NIV

These two verses give us a better understanding of *how* we can effectively "pass it on".

The transfer process of discipleship starts with a "father's love." ("You then, my son.")

Are you starting to hear the emotion in Paul's words? Here he is, perhaps days away from being decapitated, and he is writing his last words to his beloved son in the faith. Bet your bottom dollar that there is something extra motivating to Timothy as he reads these words "you then, my son." This short phrase speaks of intimacy; of a special depth of relationship built over time. And even in these four words we pick up a hint that something important is about to follow.

After the introductory remarks of chapter one, it's as if Paul draws a breath and says, "Okay, son, now let's get down to some important matters." Relationship is reaffirmed. But with relationship also comes responsibility. It reminds us of the scene from Old Yeller where the dad pulls his son aside to say something to the effect of, "I have to leave for a few weeks, so now then son, you are the man of the house."

Did you ever have this kind of personal blessing or paternal charge from your dad or a father figure? Or for you ladies, perhaps you received this from your mother, or a grandmother. Successfully passing the baton of discipleship starts with the love that is inherent in a healthy family.

Spend some time reinforcing your "family" connection to God. Make a brief comment on what you read from each passage and the significance it can have on our relationship to God, our Father.

- *John 1:12*

- *Romans 8:15-17*

- *Ephesians 5:1*

- *1 John 3:1-2a*

- *1 John 5:2*

The next critical step of passing it on rests firmly on the basics. ("be strong in the grace that is in Jesus Christ")

Paul knew well his power source. There is great strength in grace. "Strong" is the Greek word *endunamos.* It means to empower, enable or increase in strength. Paul often refers to the enabling and empowering strength of grace. In fact the strength of grace overcomes the fragility of our excuses when it comes to discipleship.

Here is the most commonly heard excuse. "I just don't think I can." And here is how Paul would respond.

> [9]But he said to me, "My grace is sufficient for you, for my power is made perfect in weakness." Therefore I will boast all the more gladly about my weaknesses, so that power of Christ may rest on me. [10]For the sake of Christ, then, I am content with weaknesses, insults, hardships, persecutions, and calamities. For when I am weak, then I am strong.
>
> 2 Corinthians 12:9-10 ESV

Grace offers strength in our every weakness. When we don't think we have what it takes to accomplish a God-given task, it's God's grace that provides that which we lack. In fact it's during those moments when we can't that God's grace shines brightest to show us, with God's help, we can. The NLT translates it this way: "My grace is all you need. My power works best in your weakness."

Our ability to disciple others is grace-based. Gordon Fee writes, "Though it is true that grace is the means by which we are saved and by which we are enabled to walk in God's will, it is also true that the same grace is the sphere in which all Christian life is lived."[17] If we want to excel in passing on the baton of discipleship, let's learn to live in the basic sphere of God's grace.

Here is another excuse we might offer to avoid taking the baton of disciple-making: "I am not sure what to say." Does the strength of God's grace help us overcome this excuse? Listen to what Paul has to say about that:

> Let your conversation be always full of grace, seasoned with salt, so that you may know how to answer everyone.
>
> Colossians 4:6 NIV

It's God's grace that provides the strength of both wisdom and flavor to our words. You can never go wrong by emphasizing God's grace in the things you say and how you say them. I had a former pastor who used to say, "If you are going to error, error on the side of grace." Instead of harsh words, use gracious words. If you aren't sure exactly what to say, call on God's grace, his unmerited favor - and see if he doesn't come through.

Here is a third potential excuse. "I am a little (actually a lot) afraid." The author of Hebrews encourages us to go to the throne of grace to draw upon the needed strength when weakened by fear or anxiety.

16 Let us then approach God's throne of grace with confidence, so that we may receive mercy and find grace to help us in our time of need.

Hebrews 4:16 NIV

Oh, to receive mercy and grace in our time of need! What a benefit this is. In those times when we might feel battered about by the unknown; unsure of where a discipleship challenge may take us, it is during these times when both mercy and grace show up together as they so often do.

"So then, my son, be strong in the grace that is in Christ Jesus."

2 Timothy 2:1 NIV

Mentally chew on the important basic of grace. How would you answer these questions? Fill in the blanks.

Without grace empowered discipleship all we have is ______________________________________.

The most effective disciple maker depends on grace because ______________________________.

The next step of passing on the discipleship baton involves verbal and listening skills ("and the things you have heard me say in the process of many witnesses").

Look back at the emphasis Paul has already placed on the verbal component.

> "remember you in my prayers" (1:3 NLT) Paul is praying for his disciples.
>
> "don't be ashamed to tell others" (1:8 NLT) Paul encourages Timothy to speak up and tell the story of Christ.
>
> "preacher, apostle, and teacher" (1:11 NLT) All three of these roles call for verbal skills. If you want to be an apostle, preacher or teacher, you can't just be the strong silent type. You have to open your mouth - and the same can be said for disciple-makers.

And don't confuse effective verbal skills with just getting up and giving a speech. The best disciple-makers are those who connect. Perhaps "connection skills" would be the better way to say it. Author John Maxwell writes, "Connection is the ability to identify with people and relate to them in a way that increases your influence with them.[18] The best communicators are the best connectors."[19]

But opening our mouth is just one side of communicating and connecting. The other important side is our listening skills ("the things you have heard me say"). A guide led a touring group through Israel and if he thought that the group's attention was starting to wane he would ask, "Are you listening or just hearing?" pointing out the significance of really letting the words sink deep (listening) rather than just bounce of our ear drums (hearing). If we want to become effective in passing the baton of faith, we have to be a good listener. Here are three ways to improve this kind of listening (both to others and to God.)

1. Listen with a hungry ear. Be eager to learn. (See Psalm 119:33-40)

2. Listen with a humble ear. Don't let a fat head close your eardrum. Above all, be attentive to what God might be telling you. (See Psalm 40:4)

3. Listen with a "hunch" ear. This is that sixth sense that seeks to read between the lines to what isn't quite said with the words of others. And better than this sixth sense is listening with the Holy Spirit's influence to understand. (1 John 4:6)

The next critical step to passing the disciple baton on to others requires trust. ("entrust to reliable men")

Here is where the rubber meets the road and where the baton of discipleship leaves the hand. "Entrust" means to place alongside or by implication to deposit (as a trust or for protection); to commit, set before or commend. We can't force entrusting. In the transfer process there is a letting go by the disciple-maker, much like the stage we get to as parents when we need to let go of our kids and watch as they start to make decisions and take actions by themselves. Like our kids, others will never mature if we keep doing everything for them.

Of course, it is hard to let go. We like the control. We are more experienced. We frankly know what we are doing, and passing on something as important as discipleship to another requires faith on the one transferring. And that is why it is important to remember the quality that Paul mentions here. "Reliable". Trustworthy. Proven. Paul wasn't entrusting the gospel to just anyone. He instructs Timothy to look to those who are reliable. We use the acronym "FAT" – faithful, available, teachable. Before you entrust and release the baton, make sure your potential new disciple is "FAT."

How do we effectively pass on the baton of faith? It starts with relationship; it depends on the basics of grace; it involves verbal and listening skills; it takes trust. And finally, it requires competency to teach ("who will also be qualified to teach others."). At this point the student is now the teacher. Someone has said, "A great teacher has always been measured by the number of students who have surpassed him." And a great disciple-maker will be measured by the number of disciples who make other disciples.

Now when it comes to this competency to teach it's important not to confuse the traditional form of teaching with discipleship. This chart emphasizes the distinction between teaching and discipleship

TEACHING	DISCIPLESHIP
Monologue	Interaction
Emphasis on the teacher	Emphasis on the learner
Dispense information	Expect transformation
Test of facts	Test of maturity
Curriculum based	Relationship based
Classroom	Life
Impress (from a distance)	Impact (up close)

Right now - who comes to your mind as one of your favorite teachers? Why? My bet is that your favorite teachers were ones who specialized on the discipleship column. These names and faces were the teachers who made a difference. They passed on what they possessed - and it could have been something a lot more important than what can be measured on a SAT score. Jesus didn't say "go and make teachers" he said, "Go and make disciples." The one who knows how to teach, in a discipleship manner, will be the one who develops successful men and women.

Passing the baton of discipleship to the next generation is God's plan. Let's summarize the importance of this section with an acronym PASS.

P - **P**lace Christ first and foremost. Remember, we are intentionally trying to multiply Christ-like followers. Keep Him prominent. "Follow me as I follow Christ." We can't pass on what we don't possess - so make sure you possess a constantly growing relationship with your Savior.

A - **A**bove all, relationships. "My beloved child", "my son", "join with me", "us" - these are all relationship laden words. Don't over emphasize curriculum – focus on building relationship – first on a relationship with Jesus and then between disciple-maker and disciple. God-centered, grace-filled relationships.

S - **S**tress transformation, not information. Fan your gift, follow the pattern, guard the deposit. The best teacher is the one who never stops learning and who wants to see a disciple transformed by the Word of God.

S - **S**trive for multiplication. Entrust others, who will be able to teach others also. We wouldn't be here had it not been for the faith of others. Discipleship has not happened until multiplication has taken place. Make disciples who will make disciples!

Make the pass. Get the baton of discipleship securely into another's hand. When you do, you'll discover the significance and satisfaction of knowing you've played an important role in building God's kingdom.

DEEPER WALK QUESTIONS

Why is the baton transfer of discipleship so difficult? Based on where you are now in your discipleship walk, what obstacles would you anticipate?

How competent do you feel in your ability to teach? Where do you need the most assistance?

It's important to know, in this very first series, to know what is expected of a disciple – and that is "to pass it on." We need to multiply. Otherwise, we have dropped the baton. What can you do to be better prepared to receive the baton of discipleship?

How would you assess your grasp of the following essentials? (Rank each on a 1-10 scale, 10 being "I strongly need this" and 1 being "I am confident in this".)

- ☐ Understanding the Bible
- ☐ Knowing the Basic Christian Doctrines
- ☐ Personal Disciplines to Spiritual Maturity
- ☐ Defending the Faith

- ☐ Knowing More About God
- ☐ Living Out My Purpose
- ☐ ______________________________

Chapter 7

DISCIPLESHIP - 3D Character

If a picture is worth a thousand words then our next instruction from Paul is worth at least three thousand. He has just instructed Timothy to pass on the baton of discipleship, but to be careful to pass it on to those who are reliable. The transfer process is much too important to place the baton of faith into the hands of one who would fumble it, keep it for himself/herself or sit back, take it easy and not even get into the race. So in order to clarify things to a sharper degree, Paul tells Timothy (as he tells us) what kind of person is worthy to take the baton of discipleship.

Paul will draw upon three occupations to illustrate this worthy recipient. But it's not so much the occupation that is important, but the character quality found within each of these three professions that matters to Paul. Like Jesus, Paul isn't concerned with the outward attributes. What Paul is telling Timothy is to look beyond physical appearances and place the baton of discipleship into the hand of one who has a reliable character.

Invest some time to look up these passages that also point to the importance of one's inner character. Why is the "heart" so important? And why is it so difficult to assess?

- *1 Samuel 16:7*
- *Psalm 147:10-11*
- *Matthew 6:1*

What are the distinguishing character qualities of a worthy disciple that Paul highlights?

The first character attribute is Dedication.

[3]Share in suffering as a good soldier of Christ Jesus. [4]No soldier gets entangled in civilian pursuits, since his aim is to please the one who enlisted him.

2 Timothy 2:3-4 ESV

Paul has already issued a suffering invitation to Timothy (1:8) and he does so again here by focusing on the example of a soldier. Those who have served in the military can certainly testify to the suffering that accompanies this occupation. Boot camp is synonymous with suffering as drill instructors break each recruit down in order to build them back up into a proper and prepared soldier. Soldiers suffer the rigors of physical exertion, the emotional demands of being away from family, and the on-going test of resolve with each battle assignment. Ask a marine about suffering and they wear it as a badge of honor. Days spent in torrential downpours, trench-foot infections, twenty-mile runs carrying fifty pounds of gear would all be recalled with a sense of pride. This kind of suffering demands dedication.

The dedication of a soldier is free of secondary distractions. Paul uses the terminology "entangled in civilian affairs" to describe these distractions. A good soldier is cut loose from the entanglements of civilian life. Out in the normal civilian world there are all kinds of weeds and vines that can quickly, subtly and restrictively wrap around and entwine us. But if you are literally dodging bullets as a soldier, then being engrossed in the latest baseball standings or being engrossed in a celebrity brew haw draws little attraction. A soldier is laser focused on the mission before him. For Timothy, that would be his service to the Lord.

Look up these complementary passages and record what these kind of entanglements in civilian pursuits would look like in our world.

- *Matthew 13:22*

- *1 Timothy 6: 9-10*

The soldier is so dedicated to his profession that he doesn't let himself become entangled in such lessor pursuits. How is this possible? All of these "civilian affairs" can be very appealing and attractive. What is the secret to a soldier's dedication? Dedication springs from a single-minded devotion to please. The soldier's "aim is to please the one who enlisted him." "Aim to please" speaks to the underlying cause of a soldier's decision-making process. The dedicated soldier has one grid that he uses to decide his course of action: "will this please the one who enlisted me?" (Most often this simply results from following orders.) If he can answer in the affirmative, proceed; if he answers in the negative, then stop and take a different course.

This same devotion-to-please grid is used in thriving marriages. A loving devoted spouse finds pleasure in bringing pleasure to the other. And this single-minded devotion to please their spouse keeps so many entanglements (and affairs) distant from the marriage relationship. If a devoted husband finds pleasure in making his wife happy, the good-looking secretary loses her luster and temptation. If a devoted wife's constant objective is to bring pleasure to her husband, then to fix a meal or help with laundry isn't such a burden.

The dedication and single-minded devotion of a soldier is the kind of character trait that makes for a great disciple and, of course a disciple maker. Find a believer who is so devoted to Christ that their every decision is filtered around "will this please Jesus?" and you've got one of the inner character traits that are so important.

As you examine the following passages, notice how devotion/love is related to the dedication to make correct choices. What nuance does each passage point out to dedication/devotion?

- *1 John 2:15-17*
- *2 Corinthians 5:9*
- *Colossians 1: 9-10 and 3: 22-24*
- *Luke 16:13*

Paul uses the occupation of athlete for the second character trait – <u>Discipline</u>. A baton placed into the hands of one with the discipline of an athlete has a good chance of success.

5An athlete is not crowned unless he competes according to the rules.

2 Timothy 2:5 ESV

Since Paul spent considerable time in Corinth, he was very familiar with the pomp and pageantry of the Isthmian athletic games. Similar to our Olympics, the Isthmian Games would gather the best athletes and compete in the year before and after the Olympic Games. Those victors who excelled through years of effort and dedication were awarded a crown woven with pine leaves and some received a cash prize or an honorary statue.

But no reward would be received unless the disciplined athlete followed the rules. There could be no cheating, no cutting the corners with a compromise of the established order of rules. Discipline was required to meet the physical demands of training and to maintain the rules of competition.

How does this character quality of discipline and integrity transfer to discipleship? What would be the chances of success if you gave your baton to one who was lazy; who refused to put in any effort to read or study during the week; who was consistently tardy or made excuses for not working hard? What if your potential disciple didn't keep to the appointed long-term schedule needed to develop a mature faith? What if this disciple simply refused to follow the established expectations of discipleship and wanted to do things their way? Good luck with that! The one who lacks the dedication demanded of an athlete has little chance of success in discipleship.

The best world-class athletes work extremely hard, each and every day to discipline their bodies. These dedicated athletes know that to achieve the victor's crown the highest standards must be established and consistently met. Michael Phelps didn't earn his 23 Olympic gold medals by skipping practice or pounding down fast-food combo meals. Discipleship demands personal discipline and integrity.

Read 1 Corinthians 9: 24-27 and describe some of the specific ways that a follower of Christ must display consistent discipline and integrity. What shortcuts might be enticing to take?

The dedication of a soldier and the discipline of an athlete are now combined with the third character quality of a worthy, reliable disciple – Diligence. It's the diligence of a farmer that Paul commends.

[6]It is the hard-working farmer who ought to have the first share of the crops.

2 Timothy 2:6 ESV

"Hard-working" is translated from a Greek word meaning to feel fatigue, labor, toil or to be wearied. Farming, especially in Paul's day was simply good, old-fashioned hard work. The farmer had to be diligent to prepare the soil, digging rocks out of the soil, tilling the ground, carving terraces into hillsides. Diligence was needed to design a watering system for the crops. Channels had to be cut to catch and divert the limited rainfall. A farmer would need to exercise care to time the correct sowing season and provide the continual exertion and back-breaking work of keeping out weeds. And the hard-working farmer knows the uncertainties of his occupation. Drought, locust and other factors can wipe out a crop, but if he keeps at it with diligence and patience, there will be a crop to enjoy.

Solomon grew up in the luxury of the palace, but he must have known a thing or two about the diligence needed in farming. Read Proverbs 24: 30-34. What observations does Solomon make regarding the rigors needed to produce a crop?

Unlike the crowned athlete who could achieve public acclaim, the farmer never received applause. You'll find no statues honoring the farmer. His diligence was tested in the day-to-day monotony and anonymity of farming. If you need the limelight find a different job than farming. Perhaps the best speech ever delivered on farming was Paul Harvey's "So God Made a Farmer" delivered in a 1978 Super Bowl ad for Ram Trucks.

And on the 8th day, God looked down on his planned paradise and said, "I need a caretaker."

— So God made a farmer.

God said, "I need somebody willing to get up before dawn, milk cows, work all day in the fields, milk cows again, eat supper, then go to town and stay past midnight at a meeting of the school board"

— So God made a farmer.

"I need somebody with arms strong enough to rustle a calf and yet gentle enough to deliver his own grandchild. Somebody to call hogs, tame cantankerous machinery, come home hungry, have to wait lunch until his wife's done feeding visiting ladies and tell the ladies to be sure and come back real soon — and mean it."

— So God made a farmer.

God said, "I need somebody willing to sit up all night with a newborn colt, and watch it die, then dry his eyes and say, 'Maybe next year.' I need somebody who can shape an ax handle from a persimmon sprout, shoe a horse with a hunk of car tire, who can make harness out of haywire, feed sacks and shoe scraps. And who, planting time and harvest season, will finish his forty-hour week by Tuesday noon, and then pain'n from 'tractor back,' put in another seventy-two hours."

— So God made a farmer.

God had to have somebody willing to ride the ruts at double speed to get the hay in ahead of the rain clouds, and yet stop in mid-field and race to help when he sees the first smoke from a neighbor's place.

— So God made a farmer.

God said, "I need somebody strong enough to clear trees and heave bails, yet gentle enough to tame lambs and wean pigs and tend the pink-combed pullets, who will stop his mower for an hour to splint the broken leg of a meadow lark. It had to be somebody who'd plow deep and straight and not cut corners. Somebody to seed, weed, feed, breed and rake and disc and plow and plant and tie the fleece and strain the milk and replenish the self-feeder and finish a hard week's work with a five-mile drive to church.

"Somebody who would bale a family together with the soft strong bonds of sharing, who would laugh, and then sigh, and then reply, with smiling eyes, when his son says that he wants to spend his life "doing what dad does."

— So God made a farmer.[20]

The 3-D character of a faithful, reliable disciple and a trustworthy disciple maker is forged together with the dedication of a soldier, the discipline of an athlete and the diligence of a farmer.

As you analyze your character and these "3-D" qualities – what is your response? Which is your strongest suit and which needs the most work? Make a brief comment on both.

- *Strongest*

- *Needs Work*

There is a common thread with each of these occupations/character traits. All three have a positive result attached to them.

- The dedicated soldier experiences the pleasure of the one who enlisted him.
- The disciplined athlete receives the victor's crown.
- The diligent farmer enjoys the first share of the crop.

In other words there is a multi-fold payoff for the disciple with 3-D character. And these rewards aren't theoretical. These will be as tangible as your next paycheck. Don't lose track that God pays close attention to our character – and rewards what pleases Him.

Take some time to read and meditate on these passages that point to the future and certain rewards that will be provided to those whose character exemplifies Christ-like traits. How would a greater understanding and appreciation for these rewards motivate you to develop a stronger character?

- *Matthew 25:14-30*

- *2 Timothy 4:6-8*

Character matters – a lot! And in the multiplication strategy of discipleship, where the baton must be passed to another, it's critical to invest your most precious commodity, time, with those of strong character. Before you let go of your baton of discipleship, make sure that, first of all, you are this kind of person. Remember, you can't pass on what you don't possess. Then be on the lookout for another who is dedicated, disciplined and diligent.

DEEPER WALK QUESTIONS

Character matters. David, the one described as "a man after God's own heart" (Acts 13:22) understood this. Look at these Psalms and comment on what each stresses about the importance of our heart/character. How can these passages help us focus on developing a heart that pleases God?

Psalm 16:7-11

Psalm 19:7-14

Psalm 139: 23-24

As a disciple (and a disciple-maker) where are you experiencing the suffering that Paul (and Jesus) promise will come to the one who follows closely after Christ? (See Matthew 10:24-25)

A common saying in our anything-goes world says, "Rules are made to be broken." Why is this thought so destructive – personally and to our culture? How does the truth of Judges 21:25 reflect the dangerous condition of our world today?

In what ways can the process of discipleship be compared to farming?

"Think over what I say" is Paul's admonition to Timothy (2:7) regarding these three occupations and the character traits associated with each. After thinking over this section, how would you summarize the main application?

Conclusion

DISCIPLESHIP - End With the Start in Mind

No – you read that correct. "End with the start in mind." Sure it goes contrary to the wisdom of management gurus like Stephen Covey who say, "Start with the end in mind."[21] Starting with the end in mind is productive and the best way to plan. Who could imagine setting out on a journey without a final destination as the goal? You wouldn't know where to start, what to pack, or where to turn. Unless you knew your desired location you might cover a lot of miles, but you'd have no idea if you were really making any progress. Starting with the end in mind does make sense.

But for a recap chapter, to "end with the start in mind" makes sense too. So let's go back to the beginning and review our definition of discipleship –

"INTENTIONALLY MULTIPLYING CHRIST-LIKE FOLLOWERS"

For so long, discipleship has been rather nebulous within the church. But if we think about this definition there are some aspects that are concrete. "Intentionally" is a concrete portion of the definition. Using the adverb of "intentionally" describes the kind of action involved. As we set out, we have purpose and clarity to our steps. Minimal guesswork. Maximum focus. Not haphazard activity. Confident movement toward a specific goal.

And the intentional action is the on-going process of "multiplying." This too is concrete. We can measure the number of disciples who are multiplying and use this count to determine how much progress is being made. Much like a multi-level marketer can keep track of the number of participants in a particular "leg" or "chain" we can monitor the raw number of men and women who are on the discipleship journey.

"Christ-like" – what do you think? Is that concrete or not? Can being "Christ-like" be a tangible, observable quality? We believe it is. We can analyze our attitudes and actions and see the results of following Christ. Are we exhibiting more of the fruits of the Spirit? Are we becoming more biblical in the grid we use to make decisions? Are we responding more like Christ in how we communicate; how we interact with others; how we treat those around us? Could you look back a year from now and determine if you were praying more and at a deeper level with God? Could others see less anger and more tenderness? All of these are observable aspects of a growing Christ-like character.

And all of those have a direct correlation to being a "follower" of Christ. If we make progress in being a follower of Christ, we are going to be more and more sensitive and obedient to following His commands. We will take what He says and act upon it – quickly and faithfully. We will demonstrate a greater love and devotion to Him by a greater degree of obedience. Much like we could trace footprints in the sand to see how close two companions walk together on the beach, we can look back on our faith steps and see if they are lining up with Christ. Now will we ever be 100% Christ-like? No – not in this lifetime. But the process of sanctification will get us closer and closer as we follow Christ with the power of the Holy Spirit.

So if we go back to where we started and stay committed to our definition it will get us to where we want to be. The disciple who faithfully follows this definition will eventually become a disciple-maker and the kingdom of God will be expanded. When you, as the disciple, take the baton of discipleship from your disciple-maker and become one yourself, then there is success.

But don't confuse success with completion. The real journey of discipleship is never finished until that moment when we've taken our last step on earth. Discipleship is a lifelong journey with on-going relationships.

During World War II, Winston Churchill said, "Now this is not the end. It is not even the beginning of the end. But it is, perhaps, the end of the beginning."[22] And so it is with this first booklet in The Deeper Walk Discipleship journey series. You're on your way! It's not the end. It is not even the beginning of the end. But perhaps, it is the end of the beginning. And as exciting as the beginning might be, just wait until you arrive further down the road when you become the Christ-like multiplying disciple-maker!

Enjoy the journey!

ENDNOTES

CHAPTER ONE

[1] Link valid as of August 23, 2018.

[2] List of the disciples are found in Matthew 10:2-4, Mark 3:16-19, and Luke 6:13-16.

[3] Francis Chan, *Multiply*. (Colorado Springs, CO: David C. Cook Publishing, 2012) 16

[4] Francis Chan, *Multiply*, (Colorado Springs, CO: David C. Cook Publishing, 2012) 16

CHAPTER TWO

[5] Charles Swindoll, *Paul*, (Nashville, TN: Thomas Nelson Publishing, 2002) p. 333.

[6] As cited in Charles Swindoll, *Paul*, (Nashville, TN: Thomas Nelson Publishing, 2002) p.22

CHAPTER THREE

[7] https://historyengine.richmond.edu/episodes/view/5095 (Retrieved September 18, 2018)

[8] Bob Blaisedell, *Civil War Letters from Home, Camp and Battlefield*, (Mineola, NY: Dover Publications, 2012) 117

[9] Bre Payton, *6 of the Best Love Letters between Nancy and Ronald Reagan*, March 7, 2016 http://thefederalist.com/2016/03/07/6-of-the-best-letters-between-nancy-and-ronald-reagan/ (Retrieved September 18, 2018)

[10] As cited in Jim George, *A Leader After God's Own Heart*, (Eugene, OR: Harvest House Publishers, 2012) 86

CHAPTER FOUR

[11] John R.W. Stott, *The Message of 2 Timothy* (Downers Grove, IL: Inter-Varsity Press: 1973) 33

[12] Winston Churchill, "Blood, Toil, Tears, and Sweat", March 13, 1940. https://winstonchurchill.org/resources/speeches/1940-the-finest-hour/blood-toil-tears-and-sweat-2/ (Retrieved August 29, 2018)

[13] Chuck Swindoll, *The Tale of the Tardy Oxcart.* (Nashville, TN: Word Publishing, 1998) 269

[14] Elisabeth Elliot, *Shadows of the Almighty* (New York: Harper and Row, 1958) p.108 https://www2.wheaton.edu/bgc/archives/faq/20.htm (Retrieved August, 29, 2018)

[15] Question take from Bill Hull, *Discipleship: The Call to Follow Jesus* http://www.navfusion.com/assets/Discipleship%20—The%20Call%20to%20Follow%20Jesus.pdf (Retrieved June 12, 2014)

[16] Question take from Bill Hull, *Discipleship: The Call to Follow Jesus* http://www.navfusion.com/assets/Discipleship%20—The%20Call%20to%20Follow%20Jesus.pdf (Retrieved June 12, 2014)

CHAPTER SIX

[17] Gordon D. Fee, *1 & 2 Timothy, Titus: Understanding the Bible Commentary Series* (Grand Rapids: MI, Baker Books, 2011) electronic edition

[18] John C, Maxwell, *Everyone Communicates, Few Connect* (Nashville, TN: Thomas Nelson, 2010) 3

[19] John C. Maxwell, *Everyone Communicates, Few Connect* (Nashville, TN: Thomas Nelson, 2010) 76

CHAPTER SEVEN

[20] https://www.theatlantic.com/politics/archive/2013/02/paul-harveys-1978-so-god-made-a-farmer-speech/272816/

CONCLUSION – START WITH THE END IN MIND

[21] Stephen R. Covey, *The 7 Habits of Highly Effective People,* (New York, NY: Free Press Publishing, 2004) 95

[22] Winston Churchill, "The End of the Beginning" November 10, 1942. http://www.churchill-society-london.org.uk/EndoBegn.html (Retrieved August, 29, 2018)

91661021R00066

Made in the USA
San Bernardino, CA
31 October 2018